THINGS TO DO IN
HUNTSVILLE AND
NORTH ALABAMA
BEFORE YOU
DIE

CONNIE PEARSON

Library of Congress Control Number: 2021948927

ISBN: 9781681063492

Design by Jill Halpin

All photos by the author unless otherwise noted.

Printed in the United States of America
22 23 24 25 26   5 4 3 2 1

DEDICATION

To Steve, my Silver Fox and husband of more than 50 years, who is my chauffeur, my extra set of eyes and ears, my constant encourager, and the love of my life.

To Laura, Matt, and Julie who always say, "Mom, you can do it."

To our 15 grandchildren who have given their thumbs up or thumbs down as I've narrowed my list to 100.

● ●

CONTENTS

• •

Music and Entertainment

Culture and History

PREFACE

When the 2020 census results were announced, Huntsville emerged as the largest city in the State of Alabama. Three other North Alabama cities are in the top 11 in population: Decatur, Madison, and Florence. People who live here are not surprised. They see the construction equipment and crews building homes, restaurants, businesses, industries, sports complexes, and entertainment venues. The Rocket City is on an upward trajectory, and it is taking the region surrounding it along for the ride.

The US Space and Rocket Center in Huntsville may be the top paid attraction in the state, but visitors also flock here for sports tournaments, music and food festivals, and the endless possibilities afforded by the impressive number of rivers, lakes, caves, and mountains. Some of the best-known rock and country music was recorded in the Shoals, and Helen Keller, Jesse Owens, W. C. Handy, and Tallulah Bankhead, people who made their mark on history, were born in North Alabama. Current stars such as actor Lucas Black, singer Brittany Howard, and astronaut Mae Jemison are proud to have North Alabama towns on their birth certificates.

The cuisine of the region ranges from ridiculously down-home to sublimely elevated, but the diversity of the geography and culture may surprise visitors even more. This book seeks to arouse your curiosity and lead you to explore places that interest you. Come and experience hospitality that would make North Alabama grandmothers proud.

• •

ACKNOWLEDGMENTS

Many thanks to Danielle Gibson, CEO of Decatur-Morgan Tourism; Charles Winters, Executive Vice-President of the Huntsville/Madison County Convention and Visitors Bureau; Tami Reist, President & SEO of Alabama Mountain Lakes Tourist Association, and Melea Hames, Social Media Manager, for encouraging this project and giving me valuable guidance and advice.

* *

FOOD AND DRINK

DINE IN A JAIL CELL BESIDE THE RAILROAD TRACKS
AT MAIN STREET CAFE IN MADISON

Built in 1955 to serve as Madison's 3rd City Hall, the building now housing Main Street Cafe once included offices for the Chief of Police, the mayor, the city clerk, inspector, tax collector, the volunteer fire department, and the water department. Two jail cells remain from those days and are great places for enjoying lunch or dinner with friends. The rest of the restaurant consists of an open room with lattice dividers, and there is a large outdoor dining patio. All of Main Street is historic, and the passing trains add to the reminiscent atmosphere of days-gone-by.

Arguably the most popular entrée is Poulet de Normandy with marinated carrots and cranberry congealed salad, finished with Coca-Cola cake or strawberry pretzel salad for dessert. The dinner menu includes elevated fare with steak, seafood, chicken, and pork entrées; charcuteries; or a starter such as baked brie.

101 Main St., Madison, AL 35758, (256) 461-8096
mainstreetcafemadison.com

TASTE THE RESULTS
WHEN TWO SISTERS PREPARE FAMILY
RECIPES AT SWEETEST THINGS TEA ROOM

Generations have clearly passed down recipes and cooking techniques, and the delicious results can be devoured inside Sweetest Things Tea Room across from the courthouse in Athens, Alabama. Sisters Sherrol Gideon and Vivian Jefferson are the heart and soul behind this treasure of a café they began in a house on North Jefferson Street. They learned to cook by watching their mother Ada Troup and their grandmother Annie Troup. This is not fast food. After all, there are likely only two or three people who will be cooking, taking orders, serving plates, and pouring the tea. Instead, they want you to feel as if you've come into their home with your friends to stay for a while.

Chicken and dressing is a staple dish on the Friday menu, along with an impressive list of vegetables. My personal favorite is the Champagne Chicken which makes me chuckle knowing the owners are faithful members of an area Baptist church. Holiday demands for their caramel, coconut, and carrot cakes lead to baking sessions far into the night.

Sweetest Things only serves lunch on weekdays, and their afternoon teas are prepared with reservations made in advance.

216 W Market St., Athens, AL 35611, (256) 232-5042
sirved.com/restaurant/athens-alabama-usa/sweetest-things-tea-room/418821/menus/2797180

START YOUR DAY DELICIOUSLY
WITH BREAKFAST OR BRUNCH AT WHISK'D CAFE IN DECATUR

Whisk'D Cafe in Decatur will make you think beyond a traditional breakfast of scrambled eggs or a quick bowl of cereal. It will be tough to decide between Moon Pie Oatmeal, Chicken & Waffle, 'Nawlins Bennie, Cinnamon Swirl French Toast, or a Decatur Omelet (so named because of the white barbecue sauce, made famous in Decatur, that is tucked inside). Other offerings include Avocado Toast and a whole host of a la carte items. Fried potatoes are served five ways, and the coffee is complimentary.

The new location for Whisk'D Cafe is conveniently behind the shops of 2nd Avenue and a few steps away from owner Tyler Jones's other restaurant hit, The RailYard. The art on the walls reveals the owner's ties to the town from a portrait of Commodore Stephen Decatur to symbols for Decatur's rival high schools. This is a fun place with a neighborhood vibe. Great for a business breakfast before heading to the office or for gathering with girlfriends after dropping kids off at school.

115 ½ Johnston St. SE, Decatur, AL 35601, (256) 580-5909
facebook.com/whiskdcafedecatur

TIP

The Morgan County-Decatur Farmers Market is across the street from the parking lot of Whisk'D Cafe. During spring, summer, and fall area farmers, bakers, and creators of canned goods, jars of honey, and bouquets bring their wares to offer the eager public.

211 1st Ave. SE, Decatur, AL 35601
(256) 476-5595, decaturfarmersmarket.org

The RailYard is one of Decatur's top restaurants for lunch or dinner. It is near the Downtown Turtle Trail and a few blocks from The Princess Theatre. You might want to plan to dine at The RailYard before attending a performance at The Princess. Park once and enjoy an entire evening.

209 2nd Ave., Ste. A, Decatur, AL 35601
(256) 580-5707, facebook.com/therailyarddecatur

BLEND IN WITH THE NEIGHBORS FOR A MEAL
AT 1892 EAST RESTAURANT AND TAVERN

Catch the spirit of this Five Points Huntsville neighborhood when you walk into 1892 East Restaurant & Tavern and see photos of familiar scenes on the walls and take in the friendly chatter between tables full of friends. Chef Steve Bunner and his team pair the finest local ingredients with creative skill to serve this community of diners with high-quality, creative dishes and a menu that changes with the seasons.

One such dish is the Crispy Shrimp and Grits appetizer which has made the list of "100 Things to Eat in Alabama Before You Die." Rather than placing shrimp on top of a bowl of grits, these grits are stuffed inside the shrimp and then lightly battered and fried. The results are incredible.

Huntsville's Five Points Historic District has a fascinating past and is happy to have 1892 East Restaurant & Tavern as a part of its present and future.

720 Pratt Ave. NE, Huntsville, AL 35801, (256) 489-1242
1892east.com

CHOW DOWN ON AMAZING BARBECUE
PREPARED AND SERVED WITH FAMILY LOVE

Bootsie's is a new barbecue place in Attalla, Alabama, but it has all the makings of an eatery that will be around for years to come. The food coming off the grill and out of the kitchen at Bootsie's is some of the best you can find, and the atmosphere and service are over the top. Bootsie himself mans the grill, his wife Jacqueline makes sure everything runs smoothly, daughter Maleah makes the desserts, and daughter Jada helps wherever she's needed. This is a family-owned, family-operated restaurant with a loving family vibe. The genuine smiles will make anyone's day better.

Ribs and pulled pork are menu headliners, but Bootsie also serves great burgers and hot dogs. There's no slaw found among the sides, but the grilled cabbage gets an enthusiastic thumbs up, along with mac and cheese, loaded potato salad, and baked beans.

Bootsie's is only open Wednesday through Saturday, so plan carefully. You don't want to be disappointed.

411 4th St. NW, Attalla, AL 35954, (256) 344-2224
facebook.com/Bootsies-107526737794474

SINK YOUR FORK INTO THE MILE-HIGH MERINGUE
OF BOB GIBSON'S PIES

Big Bob Gibson's has been serving up barbecue with its famous Alabama white sauce since 1925 and has won countless trophies for smoked meats, but the pies baked every day are also worthy of first place awards. Jo Ann Gunner, the official Pie Lady at Big Bob's location on 6th Avenue in Decatur, arrives with her crew at 6:00 a.m. seven days a week to make the pies needed for that day's customers. They begin with 25 each of coconut, chocolate, and lemon and 10 of peanut butter and pecan, then check advanced orders in case they need to add more. Friday and Saturday night diners typically consume the most slices of pie, but Thanksgiving outpaces every other time. Jo Ann remembers one year when they filled orders for 725 pies.

Jo Ann started as a young girl watching her mother make pies at Gibson's and now has been on the job for over 47 years. The pies at Gibson's are as much a part of the allure as the barbecue in many minds.

1714 6th Ave. SE, Decatur, AL 35601, (256) 350-6969
bigbobgibson.com

SATISFY YOUR SWEET TOOTH
AT MORGAN PRICE CANDY COMPANY IN DECATUR

Two sisters, Mary Morgan and Margaret Price, opened Morgan Price Candy Company in 1987 with three main recipes: their father's secret pralines, their own peanut brittle, and Morgan's husband's family English toffee. Those three varieties remain top sellers, but Heavenly Bits, Angel Bites, and gelato in the summertime keep their workers busy and the customers pouring in. Nancy Curl has been the owner since 2010, and a new location on Sixth Avenue has increased visitor traffic. This is a store that always smells amazing.

The large open floor plan makes it possible to watch the candymakers create their confections in real time while also shopping for a beautiful package for yourself or a friend in the gift shop portion. The English toffee, a perennial favorite, is consistently listed in "100 Things to Eat in Alabama Before You Die," and it truly is "to die for."

1735 6th Ave. SE, Decatur, AL 35601, (256) 350-2992
morganpricecandy.com

CHASE YOUR STEAK WITH AN ORANGE ROLL
AT ALL-STEAK IN CULLMAN

Hungry North Alabamians have been pouring into the All-Steak in Cullman for burgers, chops, seafood, and their signature, slow-roasted prime rib since 1938, but the orange rolls are what set the restaurant apart. Those sweet delights deserve their inclusion in "100 Dishes to Eat in Alabama Before You Die," and ladies all over the state have searched diligently for the closest recipe they can find to duplicate them at home.

It is a happy custom for a basket to appear at your table after your order is given. That basket will contain two rolls per person, one is a soft, doughy dinner roll, and the other is one of those prized orange rolls with the liner paper dripping with butter, sugar, and grated orange zest. If you want a second one, you can order some to-go or choose rolls that are frozen to be baked at home. The rest of the menu is great, but I guarantee the orange rolls will make you a repeat customer.

323 3rd Ave. SE, Cullman, AL 35055, (256) 734-4322
allsteakrestaurant.com

TIP

The Cullman County Museum is only a few blocks away from All-Steak. Go there to learn more about Cullman's German heritage and to see the elaborate Christmas pyramid (Weihnachtspyramide) on display every December.

211 2nd Ave. NE, Cullman, AL 35055
(256) 739-1258, cullmancountymuseum.com

STIMULATE YOUR SENSES
AT TOM BROWN'S RESTAURANT
IN MADISON

Words most often used to describe Tom Brown's Restaurant are casual, exceptional, visually stimulating, and premium menu offerings. Tom is the energetic and affable owner and head chef. His wife Ashley is a visionary interior designer. Her blue velvet chair covers, brass accents, and numerous chandeliers of all shapes and dimensions create a stunning first impression, and their artistic daughter Kenzi has contributed custom epoxy artwork and coasters.

Fresh seafood flown in weekly from as far away as Hawaii, and the Tomahawk, a 38-ounce steak with an 18-inch bone, are dinner menu standouts. Mean Green Egg Rolls and Fried Alligator are notable options on the appetizer list. The kids' menu section is laughingly called "I Want to Go Home." Clearly, the Browns have heard the wails of many children. "I Don't Care" is a grilled cheese, "I Don't Know" translates to sliced grilled chicken, and "Whatever" turns out to be a 4-ounce steak.

Despite opening during a pandemic, Tom Brown's has been a phenomenal success, and a second location is opening at Hays Farm in South Huntsville. Be sure to make reservations early in the week for prime weekend dinner hours.

8141 Hwy. 72 W, Ste. A, Shoppes of Madison, Madison, AL 35758
(256) 715-1283, tombrownsrestaurant.com

TIP

Madison offers recreational opportunities from hiking on Rainbow Mountain Trail or playing a game of disc golf at Dublin Memorial Park to a dizzying assortment of activities at Insanity Complex. This entertainment center has laser tag, roller skating, skateboarding, rock climbing, batting cages, mini-golf, and an arcade. Any of these could be a perfect prelude or postlude to dinner at Tom Brown's Restaurant.

100 Skate Dr., Madison, AL 35758
(256) 319-0000
insanitycomplex.com

ADD YOUR OWN RAVE REVIEW
FOR THE HUSHPUPPIES AT
GREENBRIER RESTAURANT IN MADISON

Hushpuppy recipes vary widely throughout the South, but locals proclaim those produced by brothers Johnny and Jerry Evans in the kitchen of Greenbrier Restaurant (commonly called "the Old Greenbrier") to be the very best. The hushpuppies served at Greenbrier are made from a tightly held, secret recipe and are cooked using the Hush Puppy King, a machine for which the Evans brothers hold the patent. One secret to success is the creamy soybean oil used in the frying process.

Greenbrier Restaurant was inducted into the Alabama Barbecue Hall of Fame in 2015, an honor reserved for restaurants that have been in business for at least 50 years. Johnny and Jerry's parents, Buddy and Bobbie, and even their maternal grandmother ("Memaw") started and maintained the reputation for great catfish, ribs, brisket, pork, chicken, and beef. Dress is casual, the atmosphere is homey, and a basket of hot hushpuppies will be brought to your table as soon as you say, "I'd like some sweet tea, please."

27028 Old Hwy. 20, Madison, AL 35756, (256) 351-1800
oldgreenbrier.com

ANTICIPATE THE HOLIDAYS
WITH A SANDWICH FROM APPLE LANE

Bite into a stuffed or overstuffed ham or turkey sandwich at Apple Lane, and you will immediately begin to anticipate the carved meat tray at a holiday feast. Donnie Lane had an epiphany while attempting to pick up a Christmas ham at a major national franchise location almost 25 years ago and became convinced he could do it better and bring that taste closer to home for North Alabama customers. He opened in a former produce stand on Highway 20 outside of Decatur in December of 1997 and sold 600 spiral-sliced, honey-glazed hams just in time for Christmas. The hams were a huge hit, and turkeys followed shortly. In a normal year, Apple Lane has grown to the point where they sell 12,000 hams and about half that many turkeys.

Two cafés now serve lunch and early dinner to hungry folks with a menu featuring their signature sandwiches, banana pudding, gourmet apples (with a name like Apple Lane, it only makes sense), and several tempting sides. One of the huge apples will likely serve 8 people when you consider all the caramel and chocolate poured over it. A whole ham or turkey can be purchased any time you get a craving.

725 Beltline Rd. SW, Ste. C, Decatur, AL 35601, (256) 351-7803

8580 Madison Blvd., Madison, AL 35758, (256) 774-8181

applelanefarms.com

• •

JUDGE FOR YOURSELF
HOW CHEF BOYCE ELEVATES PALATES

Chef James Boyce, owner of Cotton Row, Commerce Kitchen, Pane e Vino, and Grille on Main, is well-acquainted with earning Mobil Five Star Awards and appearing in cooking segments of the *TODAY Show*. His resume is impeccable. When he was made aware of the opportunities to bring his brand of culinary expertise to Alabama while also having great educational opportunities for his children, he jumped at the chance to come to Huntsville, and Huntsvillians have made him one of their own. He opened Cotton Row on the Courthouse Square in 2008, followed shortly by Pane e Vino serving Italian dishes inside the Huntsville Museum of Art. In 2010, he added Commerce Kitchen, another signature restaurant on the opposite end of the block from Cotton Row. Most recently, he ventured into Madison with Grille on Main in the Village of Providence.

Diners to any of Boyce's restaurants can expect an outstanding meal with impeccable service in an elegant atmosphere. His menus reflect his mantra: "Eat simply. Eat smart. Eat well." Boyce supports local farmers, and in addition to putting his spin on Southern favorites, he has put game meats, foie gras, duck, and Gulf seafood dishes in front of Huntsville area diners alongside steaks, chicken, lamb, and pork. His clever Peanut Butter and Jelly in Phyllo dessert is one you won't find anywhere else.

Cotton Row

100 South Side Sq., Huntsville, AL 35801
(256) 382-9500, cottonrowrestaurant.com

Pane e Vino

300 Church St. SW, Huntsville, AL 35801
(256) 533-1180, paneevinopizzeria.com

Commerce Kitchen

300 Franklin St. SE, Huntsville, AL 35801
(256) 382-6622, thecommercekitchen.com

Grille on Main

445 Providence Main St. NW, Huntsville, AL 35806
(256) 829-5858, grilleonmainhsv.com

COOL OFF
WITH AN UPSIDE-DOWN BANANA SPLIT AT KREME DELITE IN ATHENS

From its beginning in 1951, Kreme Delite in Athens was one of the first eateries in North Alabama to offer soft-serve ice cream, and their version is made with real cream and sugar. Park in one of the few spaces in front or park across the street, then go to a walk-up window to place your order and wait while it is prepared on the spot. Chili dogs, shakes, and dipped cones are frequent requests, but the signature item is an upside-down banana split served in a cup.

Kreme Delite is a familiar icon in Athens, so much so that it was featured in rock star Brittany Howard's Grammy award-winning single "Stay High." Generations have made a stop at Kreme Delite part of their Athens experience, and I highly recommend it for the superior ice cream and chance to glimpse hometown life in the Deep South.

401 W Washington St., Athens, AL 35611, (256) 232-9130
facebook.com/Kreme-Delite-111657128871882

TIP
A colorful mural of Brittany Howard can be seen
in Merchant's Alley a few blocks from Kreme Delite on Jefferson Street.

CONNECT HARTSELLE HISTORY AND GREAT FOOD
AT THE FREIGHT HOUSE

Located within a few feet of the tracks along Railroad Street in Hartselle, the Freight House Restaurant is in a perfect place for seeing and hearing the dozens of trains that pass through the town on any given day while enjoying such entrées as L & N Chef Salad, HOBO Plate, Train Masters Ribeye, Choo Choo Shrimp, Depot Burger, and much more. The homemade cakes are in high demand, and children love the train-shaped sugar cookies.

The building is an old L & N freight terminal complete with vintage wood floors, original brick walls, a large fireplace, and a player piano for good measure. Hartselle owes its existence to the construction of the North and South Railroad in 1869. It was named after one of the railroad's owners, George Hartsell (no "e" on the end of his name) and founded in 1870, one year after the tracks were completed. It seems fitting to feel the vibration of the trains rumbling past and hear the loud whistles while you eat.

200 Railroad St. SE, Hartselle, AL 35640, (256) 773-4600
freighthousehartselle.com

TIP

Peace-In-The-Country Inn in Hartselle offers affordable lodging to military veterans and those in Christian ministry. 52 Blowing Springs Rd., Hartselle, AL 35640, (256) 773-4319, pamvas.org

EAT TOMATO PIE
IN A QUIRKY SETTING
AT WILDFLOWER CAFÉ IN MENTONE

A recipe suggested by a customer and an owner with a free spirit have transformed Wildflower Café in Mentone into a destination restaurant with a menu item that is a staple on Alabama Tourism's list of "100 Dishes to Eat in Alabama Before You Die." With a slogan of "From soul food to whole food," owner L.C. Moon is committed to using all-natural ingredients and refuses to fry anything. Vegans, vegetarians, and health-conscious diners of all types will find plenty to enjoy at Wildflower Café, but the burgers are outstanding, too. The artwork, jewelry, soaps, candles, and pottery from local artists and crafters on display in the country store area provide interesting treasures to browse while you wait for your table. The rough wood floors of the 120-year-old house, combined with eclectic lamps on the tables, live music, and abundant nature outside create a cozy, casual place visitors drive from miles away to experience. Tomato Pie is available year-round, and Moon branches out to use it in tomato pie burgers, tomato pie pasta, and even tomato pie salad.

6007 AL Hwy. 117, Mentone, AL 35984, (256) 634-0066
mentonewildflower.com

FEED YOUR SOUL
WITH MENNONITE RECIPES

As you travel down Highway 157 in south Morgan County, you'll begin to see Bible verses on mailboxes and yard signs and know you've entered an area of Mennonite homes and farms. This group of Mennonites makes a living by farming and producing storage buildings and gazebos, but two families focus on baking and cooking for their eager customers.

At the Dutch Oven Bakery, you can peer into the spotless kitchen to see people in traditional Mennonite clothing mixing, kneading, and pouring batter. When their recipe results are finished, they are packaged and taken to the shelves for purchase. Cakes, pies, breads, brownies, cookies, and granola are available, and a full-service deli was added recently.

The Old Cookstove is an all-you-can-eat buffet restaurant with warming tables brimming full of meats and vegetables; a small salad bar; desserts, including homemade ice cream; and beverages are offered for one set price. There are no menus. Dinner only is prepared on Thursday, but you can enjoy lunch or dinner on Friday and Saturday.

The two businesses are only about 4 miles apart.

Dutch Oven Bakery
1205 Evergreen Rd.
Falkville, AL 35622
(256) 462-3988

The Old Cookstove
89 Reeder Rd.
Danville, AL 35619
(256) 462-1151

oldcookstove.com

FEAST ON WILD GAME
AT BAMA BUCKS NEAR BOAZ

You will see wild animals grazing before you reach the front door of Bama Bucks Steak House and Wild Game Restaurant in Sardis City, right outside of Boaz, Alabama. Your children or grandchildren will love watching for the black bear, bison, antelope, deer, elk, camels, and ostriches in the animal park and will look closely at the working beehive inside the general store. The older generation can admire the vintage vehicles on the grounds and will enjoy browsing in the antique barn. Everyone will appreciate the immaculate landscaping and will find something pleasing on the menu.

Steaks, burgers, chicken, fries, and mac & cheese are available for the less adventurous eaters, but the specialties are elk steak, roasted pheasant, bison ribeye, deer tenderloin, and grilled quail. Bama Bucks opened in 1998 and lives up to its motto—"Taking life by the horns."

292 Bryant Rd., Sardis City, AL 35956, (256) 281-9234
bama-bucks.com

FILL YOUR PLATE AT MILDRED'S IN ARDMORE
BEFORE CROSSING THE STATE LINE

Just a few miles east off the last exit on I-65 before crossing the state line into Tennessee, you'll find Mildred's Restaurant in Ardmore, Alabama, with a buffet worth the detour. In fact, BuzzFeed included it in a list of "25 of the Most Popular Local Buffets in America." Open seven days a week, Mildred's faithful customers come for miles for her fried chicken and fried green tomatoes. The updates on her Facebook page list the specifics, but your favorites are sure to be included along with a salad bar, desserts, and tea, coffee, or water. A la carte items are available, but the vast majority choose the buffet.

Mildred's Restaurant is casual and welcoming with a family atmosphere. Mildred knows what good, simple, stick-to-your-ribs cooking is all about. Her daddy was a sharecropper in the area, and her mother was a housewife. They lived off the land with stories similar to those of her diners. It's a feel-good place.

27926 Main St., Ardmore, AL 35739, (256) 423-7272
mildredsrestaurants.com

ORDER A DOUBLE SCOOP
OF ORANGE PINEAPPLE ICE CREAM
AT TROWBRIDGE'S IN FLORENCE

One lick and you'll understand why orange pineapple is the signature flavor at Trowbridge's Ice Cream & Sandwich Bar on Court Street in Florence. The recipe also earned accolades making it one of the "100 Dishes to Eat in Alabama." There are about 20 flavors of ice cream on the menu, alongside sandwiches, hot dogs, sodas, and shakes. The chicken salad sandwiches are almost as popular as the orange pineapple ice cream. The prices are a huge plus for families.

Families, in fact, are central to Trowbridge's success. This business has stayed in the Trowbridge family from its opening in this same location in 1918 and has been in continuous operation ever since. It is unassuming outside and inside but is committed to good service and to preparing food people enjoy.

It's a common sight to see grandparents bring in their grandchildren and tell them they came to Trowbridge's when they were their age. The proud history includes a photo proving that President Franklin Delano Roosevelt once ate there.

316 N Court St., Florence, AL 35630, (256) 764-1503
trowbridge.four-food.com

TIP

Across the street from Trowbridge's is a wonderful boutique hotel for convenient overnight accommodations. The Stricklin Hotel offers 24 guest rooms, a bowling alley in the basement, and Big Bad Breakfast on the first floor. Make reservations far in advance if you're coming to Florence for a University of North Alabama football game.

Stricklin Hotel
317 N Court St., Florence, AL 35630
(256) 248-9982, thestricklin.com

Big Bad Breakfast
317 N Court St., Florence, AL 35630
(256) 415-8545, bigbadbreakfast.com/locations/florence-alabama

PICK RIPE FRUITS OF THE SEASONS
AT NORTH ALABAMA ORCHARDS

Mike ("Peaches") Reeves and his sons David and Jackson are still farming the land owned by members of the Reeves family since 1835. All the current Reeves men proudly bring their Auburn University agriculture degrees and knowledge to the people of Morgan County, and even though peaches put them on the map, they now have a beautiful new facility for seasonal vegetables, fruits, relishes, and ice creams and have expanded to offering smoked meats in a full-service restaurant. The driveway leading to Reeves Peach Farm, less than a mile off Interstate 65, stays busy.

In neighboring Limestone County, Isom's Orchard, which is now operated by the 4th generation of Isoms on Highway 72 outside of Athens, is known primarily for apples, but it, too, has seasonal produce for its customers.

Scott's Orchard in Hazel Green has 150 acres of peach and apple trees but also grows nectarines, watermelons, tomatoes, okra, squash, and beans. They have an ample supply of apple cider, applesauce, ready-to-bake apple pies, and apple pie filling.

These businesses are favorites of the locals and well worth a short detour to get their luscious fruits and vegetables. Let them pick for you or get out in the fields for a true hands-on experience.

Reeves Peach Farm
334 Hwy. 36 E, Hartselle, AL 35640
(256) 773-9479, reevespeaches.com

Isom's Orchard
24012 US Hwy. 72, Athens, AL 35613
(256) 232-0808, facebook.com/isomsorchard

Scott's Orchard
2163 Scott Rd., Hazel Green, AL 35750
(256) 828-4563, scottsorchard.com

SAMPLE BURGERS
CUSTOMERS HAVE DEVOURED
FOR GENERATIONS

Willie Burgers in Hartselle opened in 1926. C. F. Penn Hamburgers in Decatur opened in 1927. That makes Dub's Burgers in Athens a relative newcomer, since it began in 1961. All three have loyal followings, and all have several things in common. 1) The burgers are definitely NOT all-beef. Fillers have been added to stretch the meat, probably a result of rationing that took place during World War I and the habits that cooks developed to compensate. 2) The exact recipes are tightly held secrets. 3) Onions are a huge part of the flavor, with some cooked into the hamburgers and some served as a condiment. 4) You know you have a sack full of the real deals if there are grease stains on the outside of the sack. 5) All three are known to create cravings and longings for home from customers who have moved away. According to those in the know, Elvis occasionally had dozens of Penn hamburgers delivered all the way to Graceland.

If you are someone who loves soaking up the local flavor, even at the expense of your arteries, by all means, try a Willie Burger, a Penn burger, or a Dub's burger.

Willie Burgers
205 Main St. W, Hartselle, AL 35640
(256) 773-0112, facebook.com/
willieburgershartselleal

C. F. Penn Hamburgers
214 6th Ave. SW, Decatur, AL 35601
(256) 355-0513

Dub's Burgers
400 S Jefferson St., Athens, AL 35611
(256) 232-6135, facebook.com/dubsburgers

BREW A POT AND TAKE A SIP
OF PIPER & LEAF TEA

Piper & Leaf Tea Company made a tentative start from the family farm near Huntsville, Alabama, but the products are now served in four shops around Madison County and sold in Whole Foods Markets. Restaurants are catching the wave and adding the brand to their menus. A few years ago, three siblings and a brother-in-law started taking compost and tea concoctions to farmers markets. The compost was left unsold, while the tea was sampled, snatched up, and sold out quickly. That was a clear sign to pursue their tea blending efforts. The company name is a combination of "piper," which is a British term for singing tea kettle and "leaf," which refers to the tea leaves, herbs, and spices. The tea leaves are imported from around the world, but every blend contains bits of dried fruits, herbs, and spices grown in Alabama.

The Front Porch Special, for example, is a blend of jasmine, spearmint, cornflower, bergamot, and two black teas, while a seasonal favorite called Orchard Blend contains bits of peaches, papaya, pineapple, and hibiscus. There are many others from which to choose. In the South where tea is normally iced and sweet, Piper & Leaf Tea Company is contributing an array of flavors and reeducating taste buds.

Piper & Leaf Lacey's Spring
997 Hwy. 231, Lacey's Spring, AL 35754
(256) 929-9404

Piper & Leaf Constitution Park
109 Gates Ave. SE, Huntsville, AL 35801
(256) 756-7559

Piper & Leaf Strong Station
7504 Hwy. 72 W A4, Madison, AL 35758
(256) 212-0203

Piper & Leaf Lowe Mill
2211 Seminole Dr. SW, Ste. 121
Huntsville, AL 35805, (256) 929-9404

piperandleaf.com

WATCH THE EVER-CHANGING VIEW
WHILE YOU DINE AT 360 GRILLE
IN FLORENCE

The 20-story high 360 Grille adjacent to the Marriott Shoals Hotel in Florence is Alabama's only revolving restaurant. During its one-hour revolution, guests may see the Wilson Dam, boats on the Tennessee River, the dancing waters of the splash pad at the riverside park, and the dense green woods of the forest. With an open kitchen concept, the interior view also changes constantly.

The menu leans heavily toward steaks, while the presentations, offerings, and homemade desserts are appropriate for special celebrations. Surprisingly, 360 Grille also works well for families with a budget-friendly list of kid favorites.

Sunsets are spectacular viewed from inside, but I would strongly suggest that you time your reservation carefully. Start your meal earlier, so that the colorful display happens during dessert. Otherwise, you might end up eating your meal when it's dark, defeating the whole purpose.

10 Hightower Place, Florence, AL 35630, (256) 246-3660
facebook.com/360Grille

HEAR STEAMY STORIES FROM THE PAST
WHILE ENJOYING STELLAR DINING AT SIMP MCGHEE'S IN DECATUR

Some come to Simp McGhee's for the live music, wines, cocktails, martinis, and specialty coffees. Others celebrate special occasions with New Orleans–inspired dishes served in this Old Decatur Bank Street location. Still more are lured by the notorious stories told about the restaurant's namesake who captained a riverboat and owned a brothel, managed by his girlfriend "Miss Kate," mere steps from where the restaurant stands today.

Simp McGhee's, which opened in 1986, is a few blocks from the Tennessee River and has a well-earned reputation for excellent food and a lively atmosphere. Cajun-spiced seafood straight from the Gulf of Mexico headlines the menu planned by Chef Josh Moore, while steaks, poultry, pork, and pasta creations play supporting roles. Owner Christy Hayes Wheat invites her guests to dine indoors or outdoors in a pet-friendly, sidewalk café setting.

725 Bank St. NW, Decatur, AL 35601, (256) 353-6284
simpmcghees.com

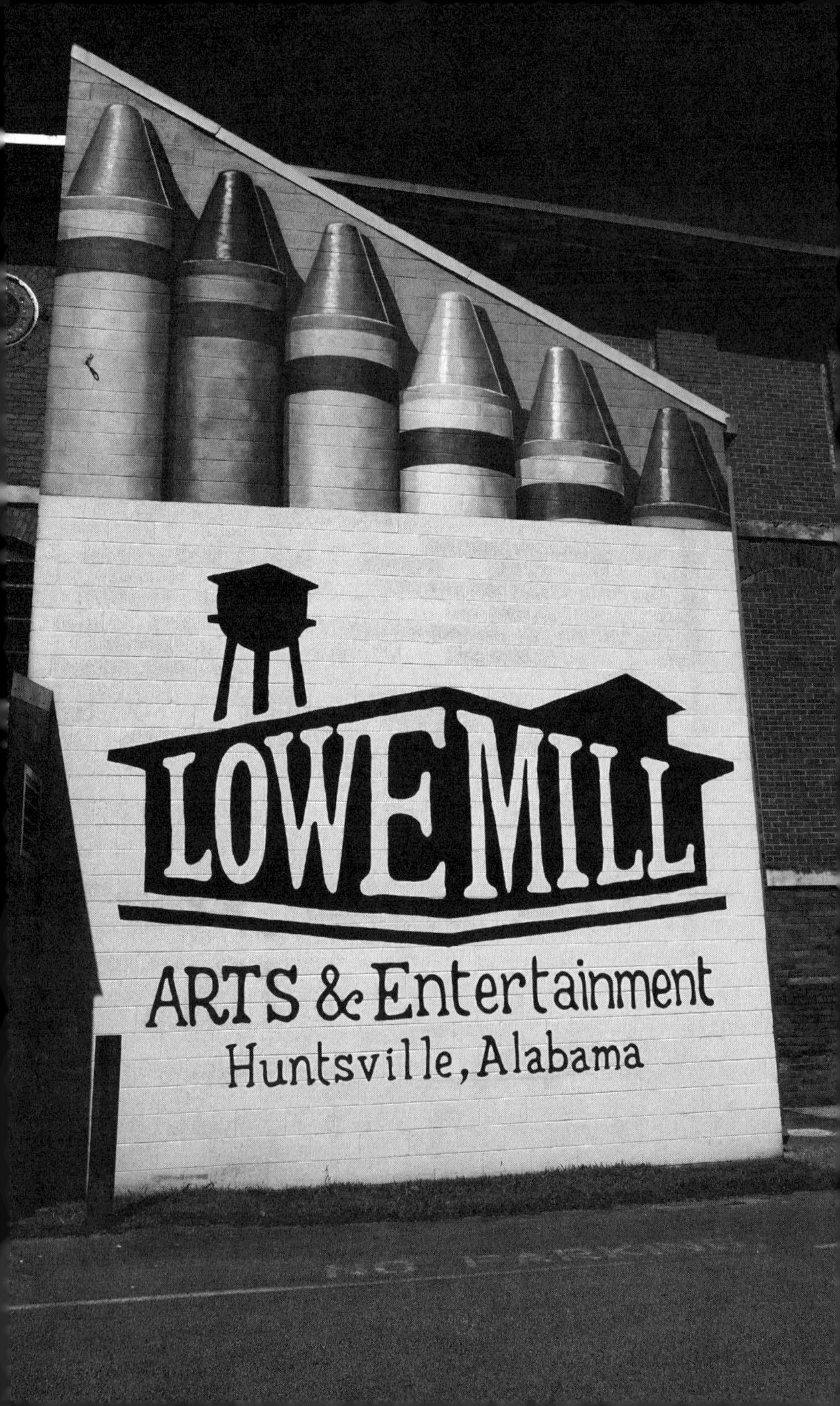
LOWE MILL
ARTS & Entertainment
Huntsville, Alabama

MUSIC
AND ENTERTAINMENT

CROSS THE TRACKS AND CELEBRATE TRAINS
AT HARTSELLE'S DEPOT DAYS FESTIVAL

The third Saturday in September is the culmination of Hartselle's Depot Days Festival, a week of events, cherishing Hartselle's past and reveling in its present. Beginning at the railroad tracks and heading four blocks down Main Street, barricades go up and the street is crammed with vendors, merchants, and musicians. Tractor pulls, car shows, an art contest, and a street dance also appear on the schedule. If you're very lucky, a performance of "The Great Bank Robbery of 1926," written by Martine Bates Fairbanks might also take place during the week. It chronicles one of Hartselle's most startling nights and remains an unsolved crime to this day.

Hartselle's very existence came about when the tracks of the South and North Alabama Railroad were laid in 1869, and its name comes from one of the railroad owners, George Hartsell. You will hear the rumble of trains rolling through the town as you enjoy the party atmosphere of Depot Days.

101A Main St. W, Hartselle, AL 35640, (256) 773-4370
hartselledepotdays.com

WATCH A CLASSIC FILM OR LIVE PERFORMANCE
AT THE HISTORIC PRINCESS THEATRE

You missed out on appearances by Gene Autry and Roy Rogers, but it's not too late to catch a classic film, children's theater performance, or appearances by traveling orchestras, jazz trios, storytellers, Elvis impersonators, ventriloquists, or comedians at the Princess Theatre on 2nd Avenue in Decatur.

The theatre's history dates to 1887 when it was constructed as a livery stable, but it was transformed by visionaries of the day and has been hosting musical performances since 1919. The Art Deco style and the eye-popping neon marquee showed up after a refurbishing in 1941 and make it easy to find. Don't let the fact that the Princess Theatre is on the National Register of Historic Places fool you. Digital equipment and Surround Sound is used for films, and the performance hall has a new audio system.

Budding and seasoned singers and songwriters perform in an intimate space on the second Thursday of every month and provide a chance for the performers to get reactions from audiences to their music in real time. Check the calendar on the website and reserve tickets for an upcoming show that interests you.

112 2nd Ave. NE, Decatur, AL 35601, (256) 350-1745
princesstheatre.org

WALK DOWN THE MIDDLE OF THE STREETS
ON FRIDAY NIGHTS

Florence and Gadsden have First Fridays. Cullman parties on Second Fridays. Decatur offers Third Fridays, Anniston contributes Fourth Fridays, and Athens presents Fridays after Five. That means if you're looking for fun and a community festival atmosphere on just about any given Friday night in the spring, summer, and fall, you can find it in North Alabama. The main streets in downtown are blocked off, so you can walk right down the middle. Your friends and neighbors along with many types of free entertainment will be there to add to the merriment.

Music is a prime ingredient and might come in the form of live musicians or a DJ cranking up the volume on popular hits. Classic and luxury car owners often have their prize possessions on display or offered for sale, and you're likely to find inflatables for kids to enjoy. Stores and downtown restaurants expand their hours, crafters set up their wares under tents, and food trucks contribute their culinary offerings. In Athens, the Summer Concert Series is incorporated, so be sure to take your lawn chairs from home.

Choose a few Friday nights and watch the towns roll out the red carpet.

Court Street in Florence
firstfridaysflorence.com

Broad Street in Gadsden
facebook.com/DowntownGadsdenFirstFriday

1st Avenue in Cullman
cullmanchamber.org/2nd-fridays

2nd Avenue in Decatur
facebook.com/3rdfridaydowntown

Noble Street in Anniston
annistonal.gov/tag/fourth-friday

Courthouse Square in Athens
athensmainstreet.org/fridays-after-five

VISIT SAND MOUNTAIN ON A SUNDAY
TO HEAR SACRED HARP SINGING

Whether you call it sacred harp singing, shaped notes, or fa-so-la singing, the singular sound and effect are the same, and Sand Mountain is the primary location for churches practicing this unique form of music. Liberty Baptist in Henagar has, in fact, been the epicenter of Sacred Harp Singing for over 110 years. It was there that two songs for the movie *Cold Mountain* were recorded.

Plan your visit for a Sunday. Liberty Baptist has services on the second and third Sundays, Antioch Church in Ider on the fourth Sunday, and Old Shady Grove Church near Dutton holds services every Sunday. All are in close proximity to each other.

Singers arrange themselves in a hollow square with altos facing tenors, trebles facing basses, and a leader standing in the center. Visitors are always welcome to sit in the back of one of the sections and join in. The term "sacred harp" refers to the human voice which is the instrument given at birth. You'll hear a cappella singing at full volume with tenors taking the melody. It's a moving experience.

Liberty Baptist Church: 1500 Liberty Rd., Henagar, AL 35978

Antioch Church: 844 County Rd. 783, Ider, AL 35981

Old Shady Grove Church: Dutton, AL 35744

JOIN THOUSANDS OF COUNTRY MUSIC FANS
AT ROCK THE SOUTH IN CULLMAN

Rock the South, a two-day country music showcase in Cullman, Alabama, is the South's smaller but equally enthusiastic answer to the Coachella Valley Music and Arts Festival for rock music held each year in Palm Springs, California. The tickets aren't cheap, and the conditions aren't plush, but the lineup of musicians is impressive, and the crowds have a great time. Past headliners include Miranda Lambert, Lynyrd Skynrd, Luke Combs, Florida-Georgia Line, and Alan Jackson.

Rock the South began in 2012 as a fundraiser for victims of the April 27, 2011 tornados that ripped through Alabama. Now, 10 years later, proceeds continue to benefit worthy causes. Spaces are available for campers and RVs who wish to spend the entire weekend. Lawn chairs and blankets are allowed, but all food and beverages must be purchased inside the event perimeter. This is a must-do activity for avid country music fans.

1872 County Rd. 469, Cullman, AL 35057
rockthesouth.com

PARK ONCE
AND BE ENTERTAINED FOR HOURS AT MIDCITY DISTRICT IN HUNTSVILLE

MidCity District on University Drive in Huntsville was once the location of Madison Square Mall. That former 110-acre space has been transformed into an entertainment complex filled with businesses that are completely new to Huntsville and North Alabama. Top Golf came first followed soon after by Dave & Buster's restaurant and video arcade, High Point Climbing, The Camp with its food trucks and outdoor spaces, REI Co-op filled to the brim with cycles and sports equipment, Wahlburgers which is the brainchild of Mark and Donnie Wahlberg, Kung Fu Tea with its famous bubble tea, and Kamado Ramen. Trader Joe's, Color Me Mine pottery studio, and a massive, 3,000-seat amphitheater that will remind you of the Roman Coliseum are the latest to join the fun. If you want to spend the night, Holiday Inn is already there, and Aloft by Marriott and Hotel Indigo are set to break ground soon. The Camp is the setting for a popular farmers market on Sunday afternoons, and the amphitheater is slated to host world-class performances and events. The excitement surrounding this development is justified. MidCity District is fulfilling the desires of all the sharp professionals who are making Huntsville their home.

5909 University Dr., Huntsville, AL 35806, (256) 489-4157
midcitydistrict.com

FEED AN EXOTIC ANIMAL
FROM YOUR CAR

Harmony Park Safari is a drive-through zoo where animals come right to your car window. You would never get this close to an exotic animal in a traditional zoo. When you pay the admission fee at the entrance, you also have the option of buying a bucket of feed. I would highly recommend doing so, but don't try to feed the resident giraffe, zebra, camel, deer, bison, elk, emus, cows, goats, longhorns, or llamas while you take photos with your cellphone. The cellphone could end up as a casualty. Instead, designate one person in the car as a photographer while everyone else interacts with the animals. It can be a hilarious and educational adventure.

After very slowly driving the 2-mile route through the park, you will want to park and walk to the Reptile House, the Pigsty, and the Turtle Enclosure for more animal encounters. If you're a little nervous about dirt, hooves, and horns around your vehicle, Harmony Park Safari periodically has SUVs for rent through the route.

531 Clouds Cove Rd., Huntsville, AL 35803, (256) 723-3880
harmonyparksafari.com

CATCH BEADS AND MOON PIES
AT CARNEGIE CARNIVAL IN DECATUR

For a day of fun that rivals the festivities in New Orleans and benefits the Carnegie Visual Arts Center, mark your calendar for the Saturday before Fat Tuesday and head to Decatur for Carnegie Carnival. With crewes, parades, and both human and canine royalty, the events of the day are designed for maximum interest and participation. Leading up to the climaxing Saturday, there are fundraising events to determine the year's king, queen, prince, princess, Sir Bow Wow, and Lady Barks-a-Lot.

A canine parade and a children's parade precede the giant evening parade that starts on Grant Street, travels down 2nd Avenue to Bank Street, ending at the Old State Bank. Parade watchers are guaranteed eye-popping floats, and an impressive haul of beads, moon pies, and toys, especially if you have some appealing youngsters in tow. Afterward, leftover beads are scooped up, recycled, and sold to help the Developmental Program at Decatur High School.

207 Church St. NE, Decatur, AL 35601, (256) 341-0562
carnegiecarnival.org

TIP

The building presently housing the Carnegie Visual Arts Center was built as one of more than 2,500 libraries funded by millionaire philanthropist, Andrew Carnegie. It served as the public library in Decatur from 1904 to 1973. Multiple purposes followed until it was remodeled and restored to its present function as a visual arts center.

207 Church St. NE, Decatur, AL 35601
(256) 341-0562, carnegiearts.org

ENJOY DINNER AND A SHOW
AT VON BRAUN CENTER'S LATEST VENUES

Thousands have attended events at the convention center, Propst Arena, the playhouse, and the concert hall at Von Braun Center, but it became apparent a few years ago that another venue was needed for enjoying live music. Mars Music Hall, which opened in 2020, fills that gap by providing space for 1,500 people to hear top-notch performers utilizing state-of-the-art visual and sound technology.

Rhythm on Monroe, across the corridor from Mars Music Hall, which also opened in 2020, makes it possible to enjoy dinner before a concert or extend the evening from the rooftop bar overlooking the Huntsville skyline. The concert-themed menu is a fun touch with headings such as Sound Check, Opening Acts, Intermission, Headliners, and Groupies. The weekend brunch menu is exceptional. Eggs Bennie & The Jets, anyone?

700 Monroe St. SW, Huntsville, AL 35801, (256) 551-2311
rhythmonmonroe.com

700 Monroe St. SW, Huntsville, AL 35801, (256) 533-1953
vonbrauncenter.com/marsmusic

TIP

Two new hotels in downtown Huntsville make it easy to spend an entire weekend in one spot, dining in great restaurants, attending a concert, touring an art museum, and finding public art all within walking distance. 106 Jefferson is a boutique hotel by Hilton a block from the Madison County Courthouse square, and AC Hotel Huntsville by Marriott is adjacent to Big Spring International Park.

106 Jefferson St., Huntsville, AL 35801
(256) 288-0128, 106jefferson.com

435 Williams Ave. SW, Huntsville, AL 35801
(256) 836-7776, marriott.com/hotels/travel/
hsvar-ac-hotel-huntsville-downtown

HANG ON TIGHT
FOR A THRILLING RIDE
TO THE MOUTH OF A CAVE

Jump on the back of a pickup truck with benches and pray that the brakes hold during the ride from the parking lot to the gigantic, gaping, rock opening that serves as the entrance to the Rattlesnake Saloon. Perhaps one of the most unusual restaurants and music venues in the South, the name came as a result of the writhing bed of vipers uncovered during excavations and renovations. The snakes are gone, but the opportunity for a memorable evening remains.

The Western-themed menu offers simple fare of burgers, hot dogs, sandwiches, and appetizers, while the live music bounces harmoniously off the walls of the cave on Thursdays, Fridays, and Saturdays. Rattlesnake Saloon closes during winter months but is a popular attraction from April through November.

1292 Mount Mills Rd., Tuscumbia, AL 35674, (256) 370-7220
rattlesnakesaloon.net

TIP

About 11 miles from Rattlesnake Saloon, you'll find Alabama's only Coon Dog Cemetery. The poignant scene from *Sweet Home Alabama* wasn't actually filmed here, but photos from this cemetery were used to recreate the setting. Only authentic coon dogs are allowed to be buried here. It's worth a visit just to see all the unique headstones. 4945 Coondog Cemetery Rd., Cherokee, AL 35616, (256) 383-0783, coondogcemetery.com

---

LET YOUR SPIRIT SOAR
AT THE ALABAMA JUBILEE
HOT AIR BALLOON CLASSIC IN DECATUR

For over 40 years, local and national hot air balloonists have gathered at Point Mallard Park in Decatur during Memorial Day weekend for races, balloon glows, and tethered rides delighting thousands in a festival environment along the river. When weather and wind conditions permit, there are balloon-centered events at 6:00 a.m. and 6:00 p.m., some of which come with great prizes for the winners. Residents and visitors line the streets to see 50+ balloons that are 7 stories tall clear the treetops and climb with their distinctive whooshing sound.

Even when the balloons are prohibited from flying, their owners still put on a show by inflating and illuminating the large domes at sunset and by offering tethered rides to those who want to experience a down-to-earth sample of the thrill. There is no charge for parking or admission, so you can spend your money with the vendors lining the perimeter and hawking wares of all types. A huge fireworks show brings the weekend to a close and officially marks the beginning of summer.

2901 Point Mallard Park Dr. SE, Decatur, AL 35601, (800) 232-5449
alabamajubilee.net

LAUGH, CRY, AND LISTEN
AT THE ATHENS STORYTELLING FESTIVAL

Athens invites you to sit spellbound under a big tent near the Limestone County Courthouse on a fall day while skilled storytellers captivate their audiences. The Athens Storytelling Festival is a much-anticipated week for all ages. It begins on Tuesday with a contest among local weavers of tales named for beloved and long-time Athens mayor, Dan Williams, who was himself a wildly entertaining and sought-after speaker and emcee. Wednesday and Thursday find local school children coming to the square, and coveted seats continue to be filled to the brim on the weekend.

Past tellers include Donald Davis, Carmen Deedy, and Bil Lepp. The unveiling of each year's lineup is always highly anticipated. Stories range from scary, funny, gripping, nostalgic, and inspirational to folk tales and downright absurdities. With the aid of the large tent, events can continue through rain and chilly temperatures, but look for a temporary change of venue if lightning or high winds are predicted.

Mark your calendars for the last weekend in October and grab your tickets as soon as they go on sale.

100 N Beaty St., Athens, AL 35611, (256) 232-5411
athensstorytellingfestival.com

TIP

If a craving for catfish hits during the festival, try Catfish Cabin. For barbecue, head to 306 Barbecue. Both are on Highway 72.

906 US Hwy. 72 E, Athens, AL 35611
(256) 233-0803, athenscatfishcabin.com

23101 US Hwy. 72, Athens, AL 35613
(256) 444-2306, 306bbq.com/hwy72

QUENCH YOUR THIRST
AND FIND LIVELY ENTERTAINMENT AT STOVEHOUSE IN HUNTSVILLE

Whether you're craving a good cup of coffee, decadent milkshake, craft beer, or cocktail, you'll find what you need at Stovehouse, a newly opened, multi-use space on Governors Drive in Huntsville. Originally built in 1929 as a stove factory, its revitalization began 90 years later and now serves as an event venue, an entertainment site, a gathering spot with friends, and a convenient location for an eclectic mix of shops and restaurants. Charlie Foster's is the place to go for coffee, tea, and cold brews. Oscar Moon's Milkshake Bar has a tantalizing array of cool, sweet treats, and the Pourhouse offers cocktails, craft beer, and wine in addition to Huntsville's first rooftop bar.

Food options range from Mazzara's Italian cuisine and Fresko Grill's Mediterranean choices to El Cazador's Mexican, Bark & Barrel BBQ, Parm & Pepper's sandwiches, and Oh, Crepe!. The Food & Leisure Garden is the gathering place where classic movies are shown are Mondays, trivia contests happen on Tuesdays, live musicians play on the weekends, and a wide variety of lawn games are available at any time.

3414 Governors Dr. SW, Huntsville, AL 35805, (256) 801-2424
stovehouse.com

SURROUND YOURSELF WITH NOSTALGIC MELODIES
AT THE ALABAMA MUSIC HALL OF FAME

The Alabama Music Hall of Fame began recognizing Alabamians who have made significant contributions to the world of music in 1985. It was a dream of the Muscle Shoals Music Association and the state legislature to build a facility where the accomplishments of these famous Alabamians could be showcased. The grand opening of the resulting 12,500-square foot exhibit hall was held on July 26, 1990. From classical and jazz to blues, country, and rock, the songwriters, performers, music managers, and publishers connected to Alabama are on display.

Visiting students and children enjoy climbing inside the tour bus used by the group Alabama. Stage costumes, logos, album covers, and photos adorn the walls and glass cases. A recording studio makes it possible for anyone to be a star. Choose from over 300,000 song titles. The studio provides the accompaniment track and microphone. You provide the voice and leave with a CD of a solo or your group. This is fun for all ages.

617 Hwy. 72 W, Tuscumbia, AL 35674, (256) 381-4417
alamhof.org

LISTEN TO
10 DAYS OF MUSIC
HONORING W. C. HANDY

For the W. C. Handy Music Festival held in late July in the Shoals, don't look for parades, fireworks, food trucks, or craft booths. Instead, follow the sounds of live music coming from Wilson Park, the Alabama Music Hall of Fame, Old Grace Church, Helen Keller Library, the campus of the University of North Alabama, Muscle Shoals Conference Center, St. Bartholomew's Church, the Clarion Hotel, Shoals Theater, Alabama Outdoors, McFarland Park, and dozens of restaurants, bars, and businesses in Florence, Muscle Shoals, Sheffield, and Tuscumbia. For 10 straight days, the festival presented by the Music Preservation Society has a full slate of concerts lined up to suit any genre, singer, or instrument preference. It honors the life and legacy of W. C. (William Christopher) Handy, who was born in Florence in 1873 and became known as the "Father of the Blues" after he composed pieces such as St. Louis Blues, Memphis Blues, and Beale Street Blues.

What started in 1982 to promote businesses and improve the economy has become one of Southeast Tourism's Top 20 Events. Each year a poster design contest is held with the winning graphic used in promotional materials. Check the lineup, make note of your favorites, and let your ears guide you.

409 N Court St., Ste. 11, Florence, AL 35630, (256) 766-7642
wchandymusicfestival.com

TIP

Ray's at the Bank offers a delicious lunch and dinner menu that changes daily. The vintage vibe of the former bank building adds to its charm.

1411 Huntsville Rd., Florence, AL 35630
(256) 275-7716, facebook.com/Raysatthebank

RELIVE
THE 1950S AND 60S
AT A DRIVE-IN THEATER

The drive-in movie experience is still alive and well in North Alabama with five locations showing first-run movies to enjoy in the comfort of your own vehicle. The theaters operate primarily on weekends, and a couple have two screens from which to choose. Concession stands offer typical movie fare, but one or two go all out with hot foods and the works. Some charge per-person admission, while others charge by the carload, so no one must hide in the trunk.

When you go to a drive-in movie, you can take your pet, talk and text as much as you want, or bring snacks from home. It's a perfect combination of old-fashioned entertainment with the perks of new technology. Find one near you and enjoy a blast from the past.

Sand Mountain Twin Drive-In
10480 US-431, Boaz, AL 35956
(256) 593-5599, sandmountaindrivein.com

King Drive-In
18478 Hwy. 43, Russellville, AL 35654
(256) 332-3619, facebook.com/
KingDriveInMovies

411 Twin Drive-In Theatre & Grill
300 County Rd. 265, Centre, AL 35960
(256) 927-2855, 411drivein.com

Blue Moon Drive-In Theatre
4690 US-43, Guin, AL 35563, (877) 987-2583
bluemoondrivein.com

Cinemagic Theatre
1702 S Jefferson St. SE, Athens, AL 35611
(256) 233-0402, cinemagictheatre.net

TRY AX THROWING, VIRTUAL GOLF, AND PINBALL MACHINES
ALONGSIDE PREMIER BREWERIES

For 58 years, the buildings comprising Campus 805 were important schools in Huntsville. After 5 years of sitting vacant, Straight to Ale Brewery and Yellowhammer Brewery saw the potential and began transforming the spaces into a new brewery, restaurants, shops, and entertainment venues. The name is derived from the last three digits of the zip code, 35805.

Live music can be heard in several parts of the campus, in addition to the sounds of Civil Axe Throwing, X-Golf Huntsville, and Ronnie's Rayguns (pinball machines). Hops n Guac contributes Mexican cuisine along with a snook ball court (the first in Alabama), while other restaurants offer burgers, pizza, sushi, wings, and fries.

S. R. Butler Green connected to Campus 805 was also part of the original S. R. Butler High School campus and is now a dedicated park used for concerts, picnics, and games. Campus 805 is family-friendly and a great place to gather with friends.

2620 Clinton Ave. W, Huntsville, AL 35805, (256) 519-6912
campus805.com

OBSERVE ARTISTS
AT LOWE MILL ARTS & ENTERTAINMENT IN HUNTSVILLE

Lowe Mill began its life as a textile factory in 1901. Starting in 1932, it was a cotton warehouse, later during the Vietnam War it became a shoe factory making jungle boots for US military troops. After the war, it was once again a warehouse until it was bought and repurposed as an art and entertainment space. Today the massive space houses the largest privately owned arts facility in the entire south. Visitors to Lowe Mill are treated to the chance to observe some 150+ artists at work in their studios. In recent months, new restaurants, the Irons One distillery, and KenziB with her flowers in acrylic have been added. Tangled String Studio at Lowe Mill is owned by Danny Davis, a retired NASA aerospace engineer who handcrafts custom guitars and mandolins for amateurs and professionals from across the country.

Ten food and drink vendors are on-site, and live music is on the calendar most weekends. In order to watch the most action, plan your visit for Wednesdays through Saturdays. Artistic expression extends to the exterior of the factory with striking murals letting you know you've found the right place.

2211 Seminole Dr. SW, Huntsville, AL 35805, (256) 533-0399
lowemill.art

TOUR FAME STUDIOS
WHERE MUSIC LEGENDS
MADE RECORDING HISTORY

When Rick Hall bought out Florence Alabama Music Enterprises in 1960, moved the operation to Muscle Shoals, and shortened the name to FAME, the climb to international recognition began. During a tour of FAME Studios, you will see the precise spots where great talents such as Aretha Franklin, Jason Isbell, Paul Anka, The Osmond Brothers, Heartland, Alan Jackson, and countless others have recorded music that led to meteoric sales and prestigious awards. Recording continues today. The walls may be historic, but the equipment is the latest and greatest available.

Tours are offered on the hour Monday through Friday from 9:00 a.m. to 4:00 p.m. and on Saturday from 10:00 a.m. to 2:00 p.m. The wonderful music interludes will certainly have you humming or whistling your way out the door.

603 Avalon Ave., Muscle Shoals, AL 35661, (256) 381-0801
famestudios.com

TIP

Straight down Highway 43 South and less than 45 minutes from FAME Studios, you will find Dismals Canyon near Phil Campbell, Alabama. This is a National Natural Landmark named for the glowworms called "Dismalites" living inside. Night tours allow visitors to see how these rare creatures glow in the dark on both the front and the back of their bodies. The sight is a sure-fire hit with children.

901 County Rd. 8, Phil Campbell, AL 35581, (205) 993-4559
dismalscanyon.com

WEAR YOUR TOE-TAPPING SHOES
TO THE TENNESSEE VALLEY OLD TIME FIDDLERS CONVENTION

The Tennessee Valley Old Time Fiddlers Convention, dating back to 1965, is held every fall on the campus of Athens State University in Athens, Alabama. It is often referred to as "The Granddaddy of Mid-South Fiddlers Conventions." Fans and performers of bluegrass, country, and mountain music converge, and banjos, mandolins, dulcimers, guitars, harmonicas, and dobros play in perfect harmony while buck dancers click their heels. Almost $20,000 in prize money is up for grabs, and the proceeds from admissions go toward student scholarships and university projects. Crescendo builds until the State Champions are crowned on Saturday night.

Bring your appetite and your wallet. Crafters and artists will display their wares, and food trucks and vendors will have all your festival favorites. Most importantly, bring your lawn chairs and claim your spot on the lawn in front of Founders Hall to see and hear all the wonderful music.

Parking is available in lots scattered around the campus and at nearby First Baptist Church and First Methodist Church.

300 Beaty St., Athens, AL 35611, (256) 233-8100
tvotfc.org

CELEBRATE AMERICA'S INDEPENDENCE
AT THE SPIRIT OF AMERICA FESTIVAL IN DECATUR

The Spirit of America Festival in Decatur, held each year on July 3–4, is free to the public and considered to be the largest such celebration in Alabama. People come by boat, car, or on foot to the Ronald Reagan Spirit of America Fields on the Point Mallard grounds, named for the 40th President of the United States who spoke at the event in 1984. The festival kicks off with the Children's Bike Parade in which hundreds of area kids decorate bikes, tricycles, and wagons in red, white, and blue revealing their patriotic spirit. Crafts, food vendors, and a petting zoo line the area attracting visitors while live musicians perform, speeches and awards are given, and a new Miss Point Mallard is crowned, automatically qualifying her to be a contestant in the Miss Alabama pageant.

The two-day extravaganza culminates with a giant fireworks show at 9:00 p.m. on July 4th. Visitors are encouraged to bring lawn chairs or blankets from home and should anticipate a lengthy departure once the fireworks show is over. Some say the best viewing place is from your boat on the banks of the Tennessee River.

2901 Point Mallard Dr. SE, Decatur, AL 35601, (256) 476-7006
facebook.com/spiritofamericafestival

SCARE UP DEPARTED SPIRITS
ON A HUNTSVILLE GHOST WALK

Lovers of all things spooky have a choice of three different ghost walks offered in Huntsville every Friday and Saturday night during the months of September and October. Choose from the Twickenham Ghost Walk, the Old Town Ghost Walk, or the Haunted Ghost Walk since each is different. Dress warmly, wear comfortable walking shoes, arrive at Harrison Brothers Hardware Store before 6:00 p.m. to purchase your ticket, and prepare to spend the next hour and a half hearing the hidden tales of Huntsville.

The entertaining guides are accomplished writers, animated storytellers, and lovers of Huntsville history, especially the more mysterious aspects. This is both dog friendly and family friendly since there won't be any spooks jumping out suddenly to scare the crowd. Also, there's still enough daylight at 6:00 p.m. to see the sights and walk safely.

Huntsville Ghost Walks provide an extra treat leading up to the tricks of Halloween.

124 South Side Sq., Huntsville, AL 35801, (256) 509-3940 or (256) 783-2065
huntsvilleghostwalk.com

TIP

For another haunt-filled outing, check out the Dead Children's Playground in Maple Hill Cemetery. Dating back to 1818, Maple Hill is the oldest and largest cemetery owned by a city in the entire South with over 80,000 people interred there. The Maple Hill Cemetery Stroll, held the third Saturday in October, attracts thousands.

SPORTS
AND RECREATION

BUNDLE UP
FOR ICE HOCKEY
IN THE DEEP SOUTH

In a part of the country known for heat and humidity, the popularity of the Huntsville Havoc hockey team may come as a surprise. Propst Arena inside the Von Braun Center is the site of 28 home games played each year. For a population accustomed to shorts and flip-flops, a growing number have embraced wearing layers to accommodate the 60–65°F temperatures necessary at a hockey rink and are proudly wearing the Havoc fan gear.

With Alabama being college football crazy on fall Saturdays, the Havoc wisely schedules games for Friday nights in that time frame and extends their season into April. Fans cite the pace and energy of the games, the themed nights and giveaways, the mascots, price of tickets, and overall exciting atmosphere as reasons their attendance is gaining ground. You'll find an aggressive side of yourself you never knew you had.

700 Monroe St. SW, Huntsville, AL 35801, (256) 518-6160
facebook.com/HuntsvilleHavoc

TIP

For an early supper before the puck drops, consider G's Country Kitchen which is said to serve the best soul food in North Alabama. The potato salad, turnip greens, cornbread, and pinto beans will take you back to your grandmother's table.

2501 Oakwood Ave., Huntsville, AL 35810, (256) 533-3034, gscountrykitchen.com

COMBINE NATURE AND LUXURY
IN ONE OF NORTH ALABAMA'S STATE PARKS RESORTS

Alabama boasts 22 state parks scattered throughout the state, but four of the six with resort facilities are north of Birmingham. Two hug the Tennessee River, and two are nestled in the foothills of the Appalachian Mountains. Cheaha State Park, DeSoto State Park, Joe Wheeler State Park, and Lake Guntersville State Park have attractive lodges and restaurants that capitalize on the surrounding scenery. If you choose to camp, fish, hike, or stay in a cabin, these parks provide plenty of opportunities. Joe Wheeler and Lake Guntersville also have premier golf courses. Watch out for deer when you're driving through the grounds of Joe Wheeler and be sure to take your binoculars to spot the nesting bald eagles at Lake Guntersville.

If you want to be comfortably pampered and well-fed while being enveloped in natural beauty, the lodges in North Alabama's state parks are a great choice.

TIP

Lake Guntersville State Park has a new Screaming Eagle Zipline and Aerial Adventures Park inside the park grounds. Check out all the details at lakeguntersvilleezipline.com.

Cheaha State Park
19644 Hwy. 281, Delta, AL 36258
(256) 488-5111, alapark.com/parks/cheaha-state-park

DeSoto State Park
7104 DeSoto Pkwy. NE, Fort Payne, AL 35967
(256) 845-5380, alapark.com/parks/desoto-state-park

Joe Wheeler State Park
4401 McLean Dr., Rogersville, AL 35652
(256) 247-5461, alapark.com/
parks/joe-wheeler-state-park

Lake Guntersville State Park
1155 Lodge Dr., Guntersville, AL 35976
(256) 571-5440, alapark.com/
parks/lake-guntersville-state-park

DRIVE ACROSS THREE BRIDGES
IN THE COVERED BRIDGE CAPITAL

Blount County proudly claims 3 of Alabama's 13 covered bridges and the title of Alabama's Covered Bridge Capital. All date back to the early 1900's and are included on the National Register of Historic Places. Swann Covered Bridge spans 324 feet making it the longest in Alabama and among the longest in the country. Horton Mill Bridge has the distinction of being the highest covered bridge over any waterway in the United States, and Old Easley Covered Bridge may be the shortest and the oldest, but many say it wins the beauty contest among the three bridges. All have been restored to support single lane car traffic traveling 5 miles per hour. Instead, it might be best to park and walk across in order to get the full effect.

Oneonta takes their coveted title a step further by hosting a Covered Bridge Festival every fall.

To cover all seven covered bridges in North Alabama, head to Cullman County for the Clarkson Covered Bridge, to Madison County for the Cambron Covered Bridge, to Dekalb County for the Old Union Covered Bridge, and to Etowah County for the Gilliland Reece Covered Bridge.

For directions to the Blount County bridges:
Blount-Oneonta Chamber of Commerce, 110 First Ave. E, Oneonta, AL 35121
blountoneontachamber.org/events-attractions

HAVE ACRES
OF FAMILY FUN
AT SPRING VALLEY BEACH

For guaranteed fun for the whole family without having to drive all the way to the Gulf of Mexico, Spring Valley Beach near Blountsville is a wonderful alternative. Children of all ages will love the 10 water slides, the huge 2-acre swimming pool, and the kids' water playground complete with a giant bucket that fills up with water and dumps out to the squealing delight of youngsters every few minutes. Concessions are available to buy, but guests are allowed to bring in their own coolers and picnic supplies. No alcohol allowed. Spring Valley Beach offers a free parking lot, picnic tables, clean restrooms, and grills. Twenty pavilions can be rented and reserved for a day where you can relax, enjoy lunch, and get out of the sun for a while. Qualified lifeguards keep a close watch on participants, making this extra attractive for grandparents visiting with grandchildren.

Spring Valley Beach is open from mid-May through Labor Day weekend and is located an hour south of Huntsville and an hour north of Birmingham. These 25 acres of entertainment are well-maintained and reasonably priced.

2340 County Hwy. 55, Blountsville, AL 35031, (205) 429-2075
springvalleybeach.com

FOLLOW
THE ALABAMA BARN QUILT TRAIL

Out of more than 100 barn quilts on the Alabama trail, all but a handful can be found scattered across the northern portion of the state. The contagion of the American Quilt Trail Movement spread rapidly to Alabama, and these intricate, vibrant pops of color appear on barns, reminding the finders of grandmother's quilts from times past. The patterns are often inspired by a prized family treasure and are painted on exterior grade board material large enough to be seen from a distance. These displays of public art are intended to bring attention to agriculture in the state, promote the preservation of historic barns, and encourage tourism in rural areas, while paying tribute to this beautiful art form.

Explore the website, choose a county or cluster of counties, download the map, and start your search. It will feel like a giant Easter egg hunt. Don't forget your camera. It's a lovely way to spend a few hours or a whole day.

alabamabarnquilttrail.org

TIP

When you're following the trail in sections of Northwest Alabama, combine your visit with one of the fun festivals in the area or a visit to the Natural Bridge near Haleyville.

Buttahatchee River Fall Festival
in late October
County Rd. 314, Natural Bridge, AL 35577
(205) 486-5330, brff.org

Franklin County Watermelon Festival
in late summer
Jackson Ave., Russellville, AL 35653
(256) 332-1760, facebook.com/
franklincountywatermelonfestival

Jerry Brown Arts Festival
in early March
Tombigbee Electric Cooperative
3196 County Hwy. 55, Hamilton, AL 35570
(205) 921-9483, jbaf.org

Natural Bridge Park
Winston County Rd. 3500, Haleyville, AL 35565
(205) 486-5330, encyclopediaofalabama.org/
article/h-4227

GRAB YOUR CAMERA AND A FRIEND
TO FIND PUBLIC ART IN HUNTSVILLE

You'll want your camera to take close-ups or wide-angle shots of the large and small installations, and you'll want a friend along in case you feel like posing beside one of these amazing works. Huntsville is literally bursting with public art, both in large and small murals and in a variety of fascinating sculptures.

The Huntsville Secret Art Trail is concentrated between Madison Street and Franklin Street near the Courthouse Square, but it radiates from that point. The seven pieces included in the Mae Jemison Segment can be found in Big Spring Park.

The SPACES Sculpture Trail now includes 39 installations, and their locations can be downloaded to your phone via the SPACES HSV app. You'll find several near the courthouse, but others are on the campus of Alabama A&M University and on the walking trail at Ditto Landing.

This is a great way to spend a day outdoors getting exercise and admiring incredible creativity.

artshuntsville.org/spaces

downtownhuntsville.org/secretarttrail

TIP

A stunning mosaic entitled "Cosmic Christ" can be found outside the sanctuary of First Baptist Church on Governors Drive. It has been nicknamed Eggbeater Jesus. Find it, and you'll immediately understand the reason.

IMPROVE YOUR SWING
ON A ROBERT TRENT JONES GOLF COURSE

Three of the superb golf courses on the Robert Trent Jones Golf Trail are found in North Alabama: Hampton Cove near Huntsville, The Shoals in Muscle Shoals, and Silver Lakes near Gadsden and Anniston. These courses, the brainchild of Dr. David Bronner who was looking for a way to increase the portfolio of Retirement Systems of Alabama and help the state of Alabama, are said to be among the best in the entire country. Professional tournament participants and high-caliber golfers are regular fixtures on the fairways and greens, in the pro shops, relaxing in the resorts, or giving lessons to PGA hopefuls.

The courses are open to the public, so all you must do is schedule a tee time and show up with your wallet and your clubs. Expect to find immaculate grounds and courses expertly designed.

Hampton Cove
450 Old Hwy. 431, Owens Crossroads, AL 35763, (256) 551-1818
rtjgolf.com/hamptoncove

The Shoals
990 Sunbelt Pkwy., Muscle Shoals, AL 35661, (256) 446-5111
rtjgolf.com/theshoals

Silver Lakes
1 Sunbelt Pkwy., Glencoe, AL 35905, (256) 892-3268
rtjgolf.com/silverlakes

LOOK FOR
SEASONAL DELIGHTS
AT THE HUNTSVILLE BOTANICAL GARDEN

Any season of the year, Huntsville Botanical Garden showcases beauty, nature, and special displays for its visitors. Spring, summer, and fall are spectacular at the Garden throughout its 112 acres of flowers, trees, shrubs, and water features. However, when most gardens start to fade, Huntsville Botanical Garden cranks things up another notch with an annual Festifall in September and October and the wildly popular Galaxy of Lights in November and December.

Azaleas, dogwood trees, daylilies, ferns, and every imaginable plant particularly suitable to the Tennessee Valley are carefully nurtured, and the setting is a magnificent backdrop for weddings and special occasions. The Anderson Education Center hosts many educational programs, and the Purdy Butterfly House is the largest open-air butterfly house in the United States. The gift shop is filled with tempting items.

Families pushing strollers, senior adults getting in their daily 10,000 steps, and home gardeners seeking inspiration all have plenty of room to roam, to savor the surroundings, and appreciate the loveliness. The garden is open every day except Thanksgiving, Christmas, and New Year's Day.

4747 Bob Wallace Ave. SW, Huntsville, AL 35805, (256) 830-4447
hsvbg.org

LACE UP
YOUR HIKING BOOTS
AND CHOOSE FROM 105 TRAILS

Thanks to the forward-thinking commitment of the Land Trust of North Alabama, thousands of acres have been preserved for future generations. The nature preserves and trails they maintain ensure that all can enjoy the incredible benefits of being outdoors.

More than 70 miles of public trails, 105 of them with specific names, guide hikers and bikers past creeks, rivers, caves, historic sites, wetlands, and farms and into the wonders of eight nature preserves. You'll find the trails in six North Alabama counties: Madison, Limestone, Jackson, Marshall, Dekalb, and Colbert. Go to the website, find an appealing starting point, and enjoy this valuable resource of North Alabama. Trails are open from dawn to dusk every day. Take note that any dogs on the trails must be kept on a leash.

Monte Sano Nature Preserve is the largest of the eight preserves with more than 23 miles of trails that have been created by volunteers. It is, in fact, one of the large nature preserves in the country.

2707 Artie St. SW, Ste. 6, Huntsville, AL 35805, (256) 534-5263
landtrustnal.org

TIPS

For some delicious, preservative-free carbs before your hike or to take for a quick pick-me-up, stop by Canadian Bakin for one or more of their artisan breads.

501 Church St. NW, Ste. A, Huntsville, AL 35801
(256) 489-2323, canadianbakinbread.com

For hiking, camping, and waterfall chasing in northwest Alabama, head to the Sipsey Wilderness section of Bankhead National Forest. It is near Mount Hope in Lawrence County. Be sure to look for the Big Tree, a 150-foot-tall Yellow Poplar.

alltrails.com/parks/us/alabama/sipsey-wilderness

OBSERVE RESIDENT AND MIGRATING BIRDS
AT WHEELER NATIONAL WILDLIFE REFUGE IN DECATUR

Thanks to the diligent efforts of the staff of Wheeler National Wildlife Refuge, the number of sandhill cranes spending time in Decatur from November to January has increased from 26 to 20,000. Those gray cranes with the distinctive sound and their less numerous cousins, snow white whooping cranes, attract thousands of birdwatchers every year to the refuge. In fact, birders are likely to find interesting flocks any month. Canada geese, ducks of many types, shorebirds, and songbirds have discovered the paradise conditions along the backwaters of the Tennessee River.

In addition to birdwatching, kayaking, canoeing, fishing, hiking, and biking are popular activities, but always remember that the deer, alligators, otters, beavers, owls, turtles, herons, and coyotes have the right of way. Maps and guidelines for these activities are on the refuge website. While there, check the schedule of educational events for all ages.

3121 Visitor Center Rd., Decatur, AL 35603, (256) 350-6639
facebook.com/WheelerNWRComplex

TIP

Two popular Morgan County eateries within an easy drive of the wildlife refuge are Libby's Catfish & Diner and JW Steakhouse. Both are right off Highway 67, the same highway you'll travel to see the wildlife. Libby's serves breakfast, lunch, and dinner, while JW is open for dinner only Wednesday through Saturday.

1401 Hwy. 67 S, Decatur, AL 35603
(256) 353-9767, facebook.com/
Libbys-Catfish-Diner-301791100067842

45 Marco Dr., Decatur, AL 35603
(256) 355-5560, jwsteakhouse.com

EXAMINE THE HABITS OF EXOTIC PREDATORS
AT TIGERS FOR TOMORROW IN ATTALLA

At Tigers for Tomorrow near Attalla, the well-being of more than 150 rescued predators, birds, and farm animals is the mission and priority, but humans are allowed to visit and learn about them on weekends. The animals have come from unfortunate circumstances all over the country and world to this 140-acre refuge where they will live out the remainder of their lives. The rules while you're there and the hours when you can visit are focused on what's best for the animals, and the admission price plus donations are important to offset the cost of food, veterinary care, and maintenance of the facilities.

Tigers for Tomorrow is an amazing resource for school groups but also for families to experience together. The walkways are well-marked, and the animals are in sturdy enclosures. If you want to observe the animals when they are likely to be more active, consider a "S'mores and Roars Night." These are for a limited number who are given flashlights and a guided experience.

708 County Rd. 345, Attalla, AL 35954, (256) 524-4150
tigersfortomorrow.org

SKIP THE BUGS
AND SLEEPING BAGS AND CHOOSE A GLAMPING SITE INSTEAD

Considering the incredible abundance of natural resources in North Alabama with its rivers, lakes, forests, and mountains, it's not surprising that great sites have popped up allowing you to get in the middle of nature without battling pesky bugs or uncomfortable sleeping arrangements. Glamping, short for "glamorous camping," erases the need to buy expensive equipment or motorhomes while still allowing its guests to spend the night by the water, in the woods, in the middle of a farm, or away from the hubbub of humanity.

The variety makes it possible to try many options on for size, such as a yurt, a tiny house, vintage Airstream, a treehouse, cabin, or even a tent with a real bed. Most have bathroom and kitchen facilities, and many provide Wi-Fi and cable television. All you have to do is decide on a date, a location, and your preferred accommodations. Then, pack some food, a change of clothes, and a good book. GlampingHub and Airbnb handles reservations for dozens of North Alabama properties, while Wild Honey Tent Company will set up in your own backyard or in a nearby campground.

glampinghub.com

airbnb.com

wildhoneytentco.com

TAKE THE KIDS ON A SCAVENGER HUNT

Madison, Huntsville, and Decatur have capitalized on symbols of their towns by creating scavenger hunt opportunities for young and old to enjoy. Madison incorporates trains with the obvious tracks parallel to Main Street. Huntsville has hidden ducks in reference to nearby Big Springs Park, and Decatur uses turtles hinting at Wheeler National Wildlife Refuge and Cook Museum of Natural Science. The clues for whereabouts are couched in fun facts about the town and businesses where they are located and can be printed out from the tourism websites.

This is a perfect activity for grandparents with grandchildren. Grandparents are likely to figure out the hints, and grandchildren delight in finding the trains, ducks, and turtles. It's also a great reason to enjoy an activity together outdoors. A prize offered for completing the hunts adds to the fun.

Bonus suggestion: Jasper in Walker County doesn't have an actual scavenger hunt, but they do have a printed trail available leading to all the painted mules in town. Again, there is a connection of those mules to the town's past. The number has grown to more than 70. Go and find your favorite.

decaturdowntown.org/turtle-trail

huntsville.org/visitor-info/lucky-duck-scavenger-hunt

TAKE THRILL-SEEKING TO NEW HEIGHTS
AT SKYDIVE ALABAMA IN VINEMONT

If you've always wanted to jump out of an airplane flying 14,000 feet above the earth, North Alabama's Skydive Alabama in Vinemont wants to help you mark that off your Bucket List. In the process, you might find that you are hooked and want to take lessons toward making solo jumps. Or, perhaps you are more inclined to watch others jump. In any case, Skydive Alabama covers all the bases.

Call to schedule a tandem jump and show up wearing tennis shoes and clothes you don't mind getting dirty. You'll be paired with a certified instructor who will attach a camera to his helmet if you want the experience documented. The one-minute-long free fall followed by five minutes of gliding with a parachute is an unforgettable thrill.

231 County Rd. 360, Vinemont, AL 35179, (256) 736-5553
skydivealabama.com

SPEND 90 MINUTES
IN COOLNESS AND WONDER BELOW THE EARTH'S SURFACE

Cathedral Caverns is popular for school field trips or outings for grandparents with their grandchildren. In the summer the slightly below 60-degree temperature is welcome, but it's the same temperature year-round even if you choose to visit in the winter. The lighted concrete path provides easy walking and handicap accessibility. Every visitor is required to be with a qualified tour guide who will point out features you might miss on a self-guided tour.

When the guide turns on the lights at the biggest showstopper room of the cave, its magnificence will have you whispering reverently and looking for someone to play a grand pipe organ. The stalagmites and stalactites that have been forming for thousands of years are fascinating.

In addition to cave tours, Cathedral Caverns State Park offers camping sites, 5 ½ miles of hiking trails, and gem mining, which is a fun activity for children and adults. Buckets of dirt and hidden treasures can be purchased from $6 to $50, depending on your interest. Then after rinsing and picking out the fossils, shells, and gemstones, there are charts to use for identification.

637 Cave Rd., Woodville, AL 35776, (256) 728-8193
alapark.com/parks/cathedral-caverns-state-park

TIP

If you want to explore another cave
in North Alabama, head to Russell Cave
National Monument.

3729 County Rd. 98, Bridgeport, AL 35740
(256) 495-2672, nps.gov/ruca/index.htm

PASS THE HABITAT OF A REAL LIVE LION KING
ON THE UNIVERSITY OF NORTH ALABAMA CAMPUS

Leo III is on an elite list of animal mascots living on the campuses of universities in the United States and is the only live lion to do so. He spends his days in the climate-controlled, 12,764-square-foot George H. Carroll Lion Habitat named for the man who donated all the money, labor, and materials to build it. Leo III is constantly monitored by veterinarians and eats seven pounds of meat daily that has been specially formulated with vitamins and minerals. He has a team of caretakers who interact with him and clean his environment daily and can often be seen enjoying the elaborate water feature.

Leo III arrived on the University of North Alabama campus in 2002, with his twin sister Una. Sadly, she died in 2020 after a brief illness, but her brother still serves to educate and motivate his adoring UNA Lions sports teams.

Any hour of the day, a live webcam can be accessed through the website, but it is much more impressive to visit in person. If you live on campus or in a neighborhood nearby, don't be surprised if you're awakened by Leo's mighty roar.

Cramer Way, Florence, AL 35630, (256) 765-5080
leoanduna.com

TIPS

For a unique lodging option only a 15-minute walk from the lion habitat, try the Gunrunner Boutique Hotel. Each of the 10 suites is decorated distinctly with themes connected to Florence's history.

310 E Tennessee St., Florence, AL 35630
(256) 374-0674, gunrunnerhotel.com

Two outstanding restaurants within a few blocks of Leo III are Odette and Ricatoni's Italian Grill.

120 N Court St., Florence, AL 35630
(256) 349-5219, odettealabama.com

107 N Court St., Florence, AL 35630
(256) 718-1002, ricatonis.com

CHEER
THE TRASH PANDAS
AT TOYOTA FIELD IN MADISON

Madison has its first ever minor league baseball team and a state-of-the-art stadium for hosting their home games. The Rocket City Trash Pandas, a name derived from the engineering nature of raccoons and represented with a logo of a racoon blasting into space, have burst on the scene satisfying a sports-hungry crowd and showing off its new facilities. Toyota Field has a 2,500-seat capacity and six food vendors. The Trash Pandas played their first home game on May 11, 2021. They are a Double-A affiliate of the Los Angeles Angels Major League Baseball team.

In addition to home games, Toyota Field is a venue for concerts, fireworks displays, kids' baseball camps and exhibitions, and all types of corporate and social events. The new ramp off Interstate 565, and the two entry points off Zierdt Road make Toyota Field easy to reach.

Town Madison Blvd., Madison, AL 35758, (256) 325-1403
milb.com/rocket-city/ballpark/special-events

RIDE THE WAVES
AT THE FIRST WAVE POOL
IN THE UNITED STATES

The wave pool and waterpark at Point Mallard, open from Memorial Day to Labor Day every year, are the undisputed crown jewels of Point Mallard Park, but there is far more to this 500-acre complex nestled against the Tennessee River.

The 18-hole golf course plays host to a number of tournaments, the Strike Zone offers a driving range and batting cages, the Ice Complex is popular in the winter, and the campground is perfect for RVs and campers from primitive to deluxe. The Spirit of America Festival during the 4th of July attracts thousands for its moving tributes to outstanding citizens, beauty pageant that is a Miss Alabama preliminary, crafts vendors, food trucks, and gigantic fireworks show.

The wave pool, first of its kind to be built in America, anchors the aquatic section and has plenty of well-trained lifeguards, but guests can also enjoy a beach area, water slides, a kiddie pool, an Olympic-size pool, and tasty concessions.

2901 Point Mallard Dr. SE, Decatur, AL 35601, (256) 341-4900
pointmallardpark.com

CULTURE AND HISTORY

ACKNOWLEDGE THE IMPORTANT WORK
OF AN ALABAMA STATESMAN AT THE BANKHEAD HOME AND HERITAGE CENTER IN JASPER

When a funeral is attended by a sitting US president and a future US president with 30,000 more waiting outside in the small town of Jasper, you know the person who died made enormous contributions to the country. Such a person was William Brockman Bankhead who was elected to 11 terms in the US House of Representatives and was the Speaker of the House at the time of his death.

In addition to displays about Speaker Bankhead, seven other congressmen from Walker County are chronicled in the Heritage Center. The personal effects of Bankhead's famous actress daughter Tallulah, with the colorful, tabloid-worthy reputation, are also included in this home where her wedding took place in 1937. The home and grounds have been beautifully restored, and visitors are welcomed with free admission Tuesdays through Fridays.

800 7th St. W, Jasper, AL 35501, (205) 302-0001
bhandhc.org

TIP

The Black Rock Bistro is a great place to eat when you're in Jasper. It's conveniently located on 19th Street downtown, and the menu is exceptional.

313 19th St. W, Jasper, AL 35501, (205) 387-0282
facebook.com/theblackrockbistro

BEHOLD THE RESULTS
AFTER 50 YEARS OF DEDICATION

Ave Maria Grotto, which opened in 1932 and is visited by thousands every year, is a miniature world resulting from 50 years of creativity by a lonely diminutive man who came to North Alabama from Bavaria Germany in the 1890s.

A Benedictine monk named Father Joseph ran the power plant at St. Bernard Abbey in Cullman, which meant he spent 17 hours a day alone, shoveling coal and monitoring gauges. To relieve the boredom, he started making tiny grottoes with small religious statues inside. Those grottos fueled his interest in more elaborate buildings. Using picture postcards for guides, he began designing buildings using shaped concrete embellished with marbles, seashells, cracked dinner plates, tiles, costume jewelry, and eventually items sent to him from people all over the world. Those structures were placed into a 4-acre quarry on the Abbey grounds, and eventually the number grew to 125. The first ones were biblical and religious sites, then Brother Joseph moved on to famous secular buildings.

The walkway going down to the bottom of the quarry is gentle, but the path leading back up to the gift shop is rather strenuous. The effort, however, is worthwhile. Ave Maria Grotto is a serene place for contemplation and wonder.

1600 St. Bernard Dr. SE, Cullman, AL 35055, (256) 734-4110
avemariagrotto.com

TIPS

While you're in Cullman, the Shrine of the Most Blessed Sacrament is a beautiful destination in nearby Hanceville that is open from 6:00 a.m. to 6:00 p.m. every day.

3224 County Rd. 548, Hanceville, AL 35077
(256) 352-6267, olamshrine.com

Carlton's Italian Restaurant is a great place for lunch or dinner when you visit the Grotto or the Shrine. The Italian dishes are flavorful, and the aromas are tantalizing, but Carlton's also serves salads and sandwiches and has indoor and outdoor dining, as well as carryout options.

208 3rd Ave. SE, Cullman, AL 35055
(256) 739-9050, carltonsitalian.com

CATCH THE PASSION FOR HUNTSVILLE HISTORY
AT THE HUNTSVILLE REVISITED MUSEUM

William Hampton has accumulated a vast collection of photographs, albums, and significant historical artifacts pertaining to Huntsville and enthusiastically shares the importance of them all for interested visitors to the Huntsville Revisited Museum inside the H. C. Blake Art & History Center. The stories that emerge about Huntsville families, events, and places will greatly enhance your understanding of the fabric of this city's beginnings and legacy. Mr. Hampton's stories are ones that you likely won't read in a history book or learn in school, but they are fascinating and extremely entertaining.

While you are there, reserve time to wander the art gallery of the Blake Center and admire the work of featured artists Carole Foret and Sara Beth Fair. Foret was born in Alabama and is a proud graduate of Auburn University. Fair is also a native Alabamian and presently lives with her family on Huntsville's Monte Sano Mountain. The work of both artists resonates with Southerners as well as people around the world.

Admission to the H. C. Blake Art & History Center is free, making it a great resource for families.

2007 N Memorial Pkwy., Ste. O, Huntsville, AL 35810, (256) 426-9163
blakecenter.com, blakecenter.com/huntsville-revisited-grand-opening

● ●

EXPLORE GADSDEN'S EPICENTER
OF FINE ARTS AND CREATIVITY FOR ALL AGES

The Mary G. Hardin Center for Cultural Arts at the corner of Fifth and Broad Streets in Gadsden is impossible to miss. The triangle-shaped building with a huge cylinder on the end was once a Belk-Hudson department store but has been completely transformed. Students arrive for classes in art, music, and dance, or a rehearsal of the Etowah Youth Symphony. The art gallery has exhibits that change often, and upstairs you'll find a 1,500-square-foot model of Gadsden as it was in the 1940s complete with working trains. Next door to the center is the Imagination Place Children's Museum which is especially appealing for ages 2–10. Kids Town USA contains a bank, grocery store, and other businesses in child-size form where kids can touch, experiment, and dramatize the stories in their heads.

The art exhibits and model railroad are free, but there is a small admission charge for Imagination Place. The center also hosts many events, concerts, and presentations for the people of Gadsden and is an impressive result of community commitment.

501 Broad St., Gadsden, AL 35901, (256) 543-2787
culturalarts.com

GAIN AWED RESPECT
FOR A BLACK ATHLETE
WHO PROVED HITLER WRONG

Inside the Jesse Owens Memorial Park and Museum, you will find displays, artifacts, and a narrated film chronicling the life of Jesse Owens from his humble beginnings in Oakville to the Olympics and beyond. Vivid stories are shared of the poverty of his family, of his life as the youngest of 10 children, of his quest for an education, and of four gold medals he won in 1936, when Hitler was proclaiming the superiority of the white race. Outside you can tour a replica of the house he lived in during his years in Oakville and try to set your own long jump record in the pit with Owens's distance of 26 feet, 5 and 5/16 inches clearly marked. The Jesse Owens story is sure to leave a lasting impression on children, grandchildren, and the adults who accompany them.

Picnic tables, pavilions, ballfields, and playgrounds make this a great family venue.

7019 County Rd. 203, Danville, AL 35619, (256) 974-3636
jesseowensmemorialpark.com

GAZE AT ANGELS AND CHERUBS
ADMIRED BY FRANKLIN D. ROOSEVELT

The sanctuary of the First United Methodist Church of Jasper was dedicated in November of 1921. The 34-foot-wide stained glass dome is 9 feet high, contains more than 30,000 pieces of glass, and is easily the room's most striking feature. The dome is illuminated from behind by a series of strategically placed electric bulbs. The scene depicts angels and cherubs floating in space in rich blues, greens, and golds. Lycurgus Breckinridge Musgrove donated the dome to the church in memory of his mother. Surprisingly, Musgrove was not a member of the church having been ousted for attending a dance when he was younger, which went against the church's rules.

The most famous event to occur under that dome to date was the funeral of Jasper's famous resident, William Brockman Bankhead who died while serving as the Speaker of the House for the US House of Representatives in 1940. Both Franklin D. Roosevelt, sitting president at the time, and Harry Truman, future president, attended Bankhead's funeral. A plaque marks the spot where Roosevelt sat.

1800 3rd Ave. S, Jasper, AL 35501, (205) 387-2111
jasperfirstumc.com

HEAR THE ECHOES
OF "AMEN" AND "HALLELUJAH" ON THE NORTH ALABAMA HALLELUJAH TRAIL

North Alabama is considered to be the "buckle of the Bible Belt." That nickname has a proud history to justify it and 32 churches which have stood the test of time. In order to be included on the North Alabama Hallelujah Trail, a church must be at least 100 years old, still standing in its original location, and still holding regular services. Some are fancy with majestic architectural details and stained glass windows. Others are plain, functional buildings constructed by the hard labor of committed members. United Methodists have the most churches on the trail. There is one Catholic church, one Jewish temple, and the Tabernacle in Hartselle consists of cedar logs holding up a roof covering wooden pews. It has been home to the Hartselle Camp Meeting dating back to the 1800s.

The trail runs through 16 counties. Download the map, pick a starting point, and be sure to take your camera. You'll find some in the middle of town, and others will have you humming a nostalgic version of "Church in the Wildwood."

northalabama.org/trails/hallelujah

MARVEL
AT THE COUNTRY'S BEST NEW MUSEUM

Cook Museum of Natural Science in Decatur opened in the summer of 2019 and by early 2021, it was voted the Best New Museum in the United States by *USA Today*'s 10Best. The owners of Cook Pest Control, which was founded in 1928 and has grown to be the eighth largest pest control company in America, wanted to give something important back to the community of its roots. This state-of-the-art, hands-on museum at the corner of 4th Avenue and Lee Street is the result of their generosity.

Among the most striking exhibits is the replica of a champion tree, the biggest tree of its species in Alabama. It takes at least four men holding hands to reach around the circumference. Openings in the base allow children to go inside and climb a spiral staircase to the top, and the leaves are very realistic. The large cave is popular. There are speakers and lights built in, and an actual cave was photographed in order to duplicate the color perfectly. A beaver dam from Smith Lake was reassembled at the museum. You can climb into it, and a piece of plexiglass gives you the effect of looking as if you were under the water. The 440-gallon jellyfish tank and 15,000-gallon saltwater tank are also mesmerizing for visitors.

The Museum also houses the Nature's Table café, a gift shop, and event venue spaces.

133 4th Ave. NE, Decatur, AL 35601, (256) 351-4505
cookmuseum.org

GRASP THE TRUTH
OF THE SCOTTSBORO BOYS' ORDEAL

The tragic story of the Scottsboro Boys is a story that will afflict the hearts of those who believe in justice for all. Ninety years since nine African Americans were falsely accused of rape while riding a train through Jackson County, the Scottsboro Boys Museum & Cultural Center, sitting beside those very railroad tracks, wants everyone to know the whole story. Through compelling displays and photos, the timeline beginning in 1931 is thoroughly presented. You will need to plan your visit carefully, because the museum is only open on the second and third Saturdays from 10:00 a.m. to 4:00 p.m., but you can also call to schedule a group tour at another time.

For many years, the story put a dark shadow over Scottsboro, but the valiant efforts of Sheila Washington and others led to the museum's opening in 2010. Washington is the curator and director of the museum housed in the former Joyce Chapel United Methodist Church.

428 W Willow St., Scottsboro, AL 35768, (256) 912-0471 or (256) 609-4202
scottsboroboysmuseum.org

TIPS

Payne's Sandwich Shop & Soda Fountain on the square in Scottsboro was opened in 1869 and is a great place for a nostalgic lunch. Senior citizens are treated to ice cream for only a nickel on Thursdays.

101 E Laurel St., Scottsboro, AL 35758
(256) 574-2140

Scottsboro is home to the Unclaimed Baggage Center, visited by over a million curious bargain shoppers each year. It's amazing what people pack in their suitcases or leave behind on airplanes.

509 W Willow St., Scottsboro, AL 35758
(256) 259-1525, unclaimedbaggage.com

IMAGINE BLASTING INTO ORBIT
AT THE US SPACE AND ROCKET CENTER

The US Space and Rocket Center is the best possible place to learn how Dr. Wernher Von Braun and his team of German scientists transformed Huntsville into a city with its current nickname as the "Rocket City." The authentic Saturn V moon rocket amazes visitors with its size inside the Davidson Center. The thrill rides for young people (and the more sedate rides for little ones) along with the movies playing in the National Geographic Theater are great entertainment to accompany the games, displays, and informational plaques scattered throughout the grounds.

The newest addition to the Space and Rocket Center is the INTUITIVE Planetarium. Unique to the Southeast, it is an 8K digital planetarium and dome experience and offers daily programming. While you're touring and learning, find out about Space Camp offering programs for ages 7 through adult.

It will be easy to see why this has been Alabama's top paid attraction for many years and is an affiliate of the Smithsonian Institution. The facilities, the displays, and the staff are out of this world.

1 Tranquility Base, Huntsville, AL 35805, (256) 837-3400
rocketcenter.com

TIP

Don't miss the grave of Miss Baker, the monkey who rode a Jupiter rocket into space. Bananas are often left on her tombstone by admirers and animal lovers. Also, near the gift shop, children will want to see K'Rex, the 12-foot-tall toy dinosaur made from 350,000 K'Nex pieces.

LEARN
THE IMPRESSIVE HISTORY
OF GENERAL JOSEPH WHEELER

Pond Spring is a 50-acre site encompassing 12 buildings, one of which is the former home of General Joseph Wheeler, better known as "Fighting Joe." The two-story home, which is the property's focal point, was built in the 1870s by Wheeler's father-in-law as a gift after the marriage of Wheeler and his daughter Daniella Sherrod. The Wheeler's daughter Annie remained at the house until her death in 1955. In 1977, it was placed on the National Register of Historic Places and was soon donated to the State of Alabama.

General Wheeler first became famous for being a Major General of Cavalry in the Confederate Army, then as a United States congressman and finally as a General during the Spanish-American War. He was buried in Arlington Cemetery, but his wife is buried on the grounds of Pond Spring. The furnishings and artifacts in the house are original to the family, and other buildings on the property date back to 1818.

Check the website for days and times for tours and for special events at Pond Spring, such as the Heirloom Plant Sale in the spring and the Christmas Open House.

12280 Hwy. 20, Hillsboro, AL 35643, (256) 637-8513
ahc.alabama.gov/properties/pondspring/pondspring.aspx

TIP

The most popular meat-and-three café near
Pond Spring is Dot's Soulfood. Be sure to save
room for a homemade dessert.

18152 AL Hwy. 20, Hillsboro, AL 35643
(256) 637-8002, facebook.com/DotsSoulFood

FIND INSPIRATION IN ONE MAN'S DEDICATION
TO HIS GREAT-GREAT-GRANDMOTHER'S MEMORY

Tom Hendrix had a great-great-grandmother whose story inspired him to spend 35 years of his life creating a memorial to her, the Wichahpi Commemorative Wall. By his count, Tom hauled 8.5 million pounds of rocks and handled them at least three times for a total of 25.5 million pounds. During the process he wore out many wheelbarrows, countless pairs of gloves, a few trucks, shovels, and even a couple of dogs. Te-lah-nay, Tom's great-great-grandmother, was a member of the Yuchi Native American tribe who was forced to leave her home on the banks of the Tennessee River during the Trail of Tears. She survived the trip to Oklahoma, but even more remarkably, she spent 5 years walking back to what she called "the river that sings." Tom's goal was to lay a stone representing each one of her steps back home.

Tom died in 2017, but the wall he built remains open to the public 7 days a week. It is a peaceful, absorbing, dramatic place.

13890 County Rd. 8, Florence, AL 35633, (256) 764-3617
ifthelegendsfade.com

REKINDLE (OR IGNITE) ROMANCE
AT GORHAM'S BLUFF IN PISGAH

The Lodge at Gorham's Bluff in Pisgah, Alabama, is a perfect place to drink in spectacular views, unplug from life's demands, savor farm-fresh, gourmet meals, and spend time focusing on someone you love. From its vantage point at the top of Sand Mountain, you can watch the changing seasons in the Tennessee River valley below. The furnishings and décor are tastefully elegant, and each guest suite has a fireplace, a whirlpool tub, and a private balcony porch.

Adding to the quietness, there are no TVs in the rooms, and Gorham's Bluff is in a dry county, so you'd need to bring your own favorite alcoholic beverages. No children under the age of 12 are allowed in the dining room, so clearly this is a destination geared toward couples. Several cottages are available to rent if you are traveling with children.

101 Gorham Dr., Pisgah, AL 35765, (256) 451-8439
gorhamsbluff.com

REMEMBER A BRAVE GIRL
AND HER MIRACLE-WORKING TEACHER

During the last weekend in June, Tuscumbia honors its most famous native with a 4-day festival. On Thursday, the Helen Keller Festival begins with a parade through the downtown streets. A marketplace of vendors during the day and concerts at night highlight Friday, Saturday, and Sunday with fun runs and a golf tournament also taking place on Saturday.

"The Miracle Worker," a play about Helen Keller and her patient teacher Annie Sullivan, takes place on the grounds of Helen's birthplace, Ivy Green, on Fridays and Saturdays during the months of June and July every summer, and tours of Ivy Green are given throughout the year Monday through Saturday. The festival weekend is the perfect time to shop for crafts, hear great music, watch a performance of the play, and tour the home and grounds. By all means, see the well where Helen first realized how to communicate the word "water."

300 N Common St. W, Tuscumbia, AL 35674, (256) 383-0783
helenkellerfestival.com, helenkellerbirthplace.org

SEE FRANK LLOYD WRIGHT'S EXTERIOR AND INTERIOR CONCEPTS
AT THE ROSENBAUM HOUSE

Florence, Alabama, can boast the only Frank Lloyd Wright house in Alabama, and the only one open for public tours in the entire southeast. Wright designed the home for the Rosenbaum family in 1939 along with its built-in and freestanding furniture. His design allowed for a smooth addition in 1948, in keeping with the original style, when it was expanded by more than 1,000 square feet. Members of the Rosenbaum family lived in the house until 1999, when it became the property of the City of Florence which oversaw its meticulous restoration. You will appreciate your visit to the house with a trained docent, because there are so many imaginative details contained inside. Architecture buffs will love the way the house was built in harmony with the land. Take the time to go and learn the Usonian concept and examples of Frank Lloyd Wright's genius.

601 Riverview Dr., Florence, AL 35630, (256) 718-5050
wrightinalabama.com

TAKE IN THE VIEW AT BURRITT
ON THE MOUNTAIN IN HUNTSVILLE

The magnificent, 167-acre setting of Burritt on the Mountain offers breathtaking views of the Huntsville skyline from high atop Monte Sano Mountain. On this property, willed to the city by Dr. William Burritt in 1955, you can tour his former home, learn about Tennessee Valley farm life in the 19th century, hike one of several nature trails, participate in a class, or shop in Josie's, the lovely gift shop named for Dr. Burritt's second wife. A summer concert series is presented on the grounds, and Wednesday nights bring cocktails and gourmet meals. Burritt is also a stunning wedding venue.

This combination park and open-air museum is open to the public year-round Tuesdays through Saturdays. The drive to the entrance is particularly enjoyable in the spring and fall, but the holiday decorations also attract many visitors.

3101 Burritt Dr. SE, Huntsville, AL 35801, (256) 536-2882
burrittonthemountain.com

VIEW EXQUISITE BUCCELLATI SILVER CREATIONS
AT THE HUNTSVILLE MUSEUM OF ART

Thanks to a generous benefactor, Huntsville Museum of Art has the largest collection of Buccellati silver on public display in the world. The flamingo, giraffe, and family of deer crafted from silver may be centerpieces, but many smaller pieces are equally as stunning. Visitors are always treated to this collection on permanent display, along with more than 3,000 works of art with an emphasis on 19th and 20th century American art. In addition to these, the museum has a constant schedule of traveling exhibits, classes for adults and children, lunch and learn events, and a formal summer gala. In the winter, the museum sets up an ice-skating rink in the adjacent Big Spring International Park which serves as a popular fundraising opportunity and family fun activity.

The interactive galleries, such as ART LAB and A Walk through Time, are well-designed for teaching children to appreciate art. Pane e Vino is a pizzeria on the ground floor with indoor dining or a large outdoor patio overlooking the park.

300 Church St. S, Huntsville, AL 35801, (256) 535-4350
hsvmuseum.org

SING ALONG WITH THE HITS
PLAYING INSIDE THE ALABAMA FAN CLUB AND MUSEUM IN FORT PAYNE

Songs recorded by "Alabama," made up of Fort Payne natives and cousins, Randy Travis, Jeff Cook, and Teddy Gentry along with their drummer Mark Herndon, ignited enthusiasm and created a passionately loyal fan base among country music lovers in the 1980s that continues today. The group earned more than 200 awards, the most ever in the history of country music, and the Alabama Fan Club and Museum in Fort Payne proudly showcases the band's success.

Fifty years' worth of personal memorabilia, hit records, photos, and videos are on display in the museum, and the gift shop offers t-shirts, hats, and more for proud, diehard fans. It is open every day except Monday. For even more Alabama adoration, drive a few blocks and get some exercise at the Alabama Walking Park. You can't miss the statues of the singers at the entrance. The singers still live in Fort Payne, so you might catch a glimpse of one of them while you're in town.

101 Glenn Boulevard SW, Fort Payne, AL 35967, (256) 845-1646
thealabamaband.com

TIP

For lovers of antiques and collectibles, two floors of treasures are waiting at the Big Mill Company, a former hosiery factory dating back to 1889. Appropriately, the Vintage 1889 Restaurant is also located inside.

151 8th St. NE, Fort Payne, AL 35967
(256) 845-3380, bigmillcompany.com

PAY TRIBUTE
WHILE VIEWING THE SYMBOLS OF MILITARY SERVICE AND SACRIFICE

The Alabama Veterans Museum in Athens, formerly housed in an L & N Freight Depot, recently celebrated the ribbon-cutting, attended by Alabama Governor Kay Ivey, for its new, much larger facility across the parking lot on Pryor Street. All the artifacts, uniforms, medals, weapons, gear, photos, and videos have been donated by veterans or their families with the purpose of celebrating and honoring the accomplishments of local men and women who served and the sacrifices of their families back home.

Displays cover military history from the Revolutionary War and Pearl Harbor to the present Operation Enduring Freedom and everything in between. The museum is open six days a week. There is no admission charge, but donations are accepted. If you are a veteran, you and your family are invited to Coffee Call at 0800 on the first Saturday of every month. It's a great chance to enjoy a light breakfast and visit with other veterans.

114 W Pryor St., Athens, AL 35611, (256) 771-7578
alabamaveteransmuseum.com

TIP
Lucia's Cocina Mexicana at 208 West Market Street in Athens is a popular spot for lunch and dinner seven days a week. (256) 998-5451

CLIMB TO THE TOP
OF THE INDIAN MOUND IN FLORENCE

Take time to climb the 70 steps to the top of the 43-foot-high Florence Indian Mound and imagine its beginning thousands of years ago when it was level with the ground. The museum across the street from the mound addresses the history of Native Americans in the Shoals region of the Tennessee Valley going back almost 12,000 years, long before the days of the Choctaws, Cherokees, and Creeks. Only a few pottery pieces and projectile points have been excavated from the site. Because it is thought to have been a burial ground, it will remain undisturbed. The museum, however, displays the largest collection of Native American pottery, pipes, tools, and jewelry in Alabama. Journey from the Ice Age to the explorations of Hernando DeSoto and beyond to learn about the interactions of the Native American tribes with those who crossed their paths. The museum opened to the public in 2017 and replaced an older one that had been in use since 1968.

A small admission fee is charged for the museum, but there is no charge for climbing the mound. Plan to allow at least an hour for your visit.

1028 S Court St., Florence, AL 35630, (256) 760-6427
facebook.com/FlorenceIndianMoundMuseum

MAIL A LETTER IN MOORESVILLE
AT ALABAMA'S OLDEST POST OFFICE

The town of Mooresville, Alabama, with a current population of 68, was designated as a town in 1818, a year before Alabama became a state. The tiny post office is the oldest operational post office in Alabama, and judging from the construction methods used, the building itself dates to the 1840s. The entire town of Mooresville is on the National Register of Historic Places, so a drive through it will provide a beautiful glimpse of a simpler, gentler life.

One building claims ties to President Andrew Johnson, while another is said to have hosted President James A. Garfield. You will want to stop your car and read all the historic markers and signs. The Stagecoach Tavern dates to 1821 and is thought to be the oldest frame public building in Alabama.

Mooresville, located a few short miles from Decatur, is often referred to as Alabama's version of Colonial Williamsburg, but without the commercialism, costumes, and hefty admission fee. You can drive through Mooresville for free.

Town of Mooresville, Mooresville, AL 35649, (256) 445-2590
mooresvilleal.com

DISCOVER POPE'S TAVERN
WHERE CIVIL WAR SOLDIERS FROM BOTH SIDES WERE HOSPITALIZED

The building where Pope's Tavern and Museum stands in Florence can be traced back to 1830, when it served as an inn, a tavern, and a stop for the stagecoach. During the Civil War, it was constricted into service as a hospital treating both Union and Confederate soldiers with the townspeople serving as nurses, orderlies, and helping in any way possible. Felix Lambeth bought it to use as his residence in 1874, and the house stayed in the Lambeth family until 1965 when it was purchased by the City of Florence.

One side of the museum showcases artifacts saved from Forks of Cypress, Florence's largest plantation which burned in 1966. The dining table made from a piano that fell off a wagon and the churn that rocks side to side are two must-see remnants of antebellum life.

The other side contains weapons, letters, portraits, clothing, flags, a church pew riddled with bullet holes, and medical equipment used during the Civil War and donated to the museum by area families. This is the sobering side of the museum, the part that reveals through its displays both war's heroes and its ugliness.

As one of the oldest buildings in the area, it has true historical significance.

203 Hermitage Dr., Florence, AL 35630, (256) 760-6439
facebook.com/PopesTavernMuseum

"Breaki

The artist tha
all the time

Pri

SHOPPING AND FASHION

ADMIRE STUNNING FABRIC CREATIONS
BY NATALIE CHANIN IN FLORENCE

Natalie Chanin's roots run deep in the South and specifically in Florence. After college and 20 years of design experience in New York City, she found a path back to Florence in order to build a business reflecting her commitment to organic cotton, slow designs, and hiring practices that foster high quality and excellence, sustainability, and elegance. The result is Alabama Chanin, a factory where hand-sewn and machine-sewn garments are created and where classes are available to those wanting to make their own clothes using Natalie's designs and fabrics. Alabama Chanin's showroom and café are open to the public, and behind-the-scenes tours are offered at 2:00 p.m. on weekdays. The café serves healthy, locally sourced fare, and specialty kitchen gadgets, handmade linens, dishes, and gifts are for sale. It is possible that you could catch a glimpse of Natalie herself serving her lunch guests.

Alabama Chanin @The Factory
462 Lane Dr., Florence, AL 35630, (256) 760-1090
alabamachanin.com

BECOME THE BRIDE OF YOUR DREAMS
AT THE SOMETHING BLUE SHOPPE IN HARTSELLE

With a building dating back to 1915 and a business in operation for more than 50 years, T.J. Holmes and his staff at The Something Blue Shoppe on Main Street in Hartselle exude confidence and competence while helping thousands of brides fulfill their wedding dress dreams. The bridal shop is one of the most prestigious and popular in North Alabama.

You and your bridal party should make an appointment. There will be a get-to-know-you time with a consultant before making selections and narrowing those down to the perfect wedding dress. Drinks ease the process and often snacks and live music on the grand piano add to the pampering and merriment. Mothers, grandmothers, and bridesmaids will also find their perfect attire for the big day.

224 Main St. W, Hartselle, AL 35640, (256) 773-4956
thesomethingblueshoppe.com

TIP

Plan a couple of hours after your appointment for browsing the boutiques and antique stores lining Main Street, as well as restaurants with fare from brick oven pizza to Poulet de Normandy or shaved ice.

EAT, SHOP, AND ADMIRE
THE ART IN ATHENS

Downtown merchants and Athens city officials have jumped wholeheartedly into the Main Street Alabama and Main Street America revitalization efforts, and the gleaming results are paying big dividends. Downtown Athens has become a popular destination where locals and visitors can enjoy public art, shop for the perfect accessory or home décor item, buy art created by local artists, set up their lawn chair for a big event, or order a great meal.

Anchored by the recently refurbished Limestone County Courthouse, visitors can choose from U. G. White Hardware (going strong since 1917), Pimento's, Trinity's, Epiphany Boutique, and more for shopping. The dining options are surprisingly numerous with The Square Clock coffee shop, Wildwood Deli, Terranova's, Sweetest Things Tea Room, Washington Street Diner, and Athens Ale House and Cellar. High Cotton Arts and 'That's SO Art' will satisfy your craving for local creativity, and Merchants Alley will soon be filled with murals that are sure to be Instagram sensations.

107 N Jefferson St., Athens, AL 35611, (256) 232-9040
athensmainstreet.org

TIP
Keep track of the time when you park on the square. Those prime spots on Marion, Jefferson, Washington, and Market Streets have a 3-hour limit, but parking lots a block away allow you to park for 10 hours at a time.

FIND A PERFECT PIECE OF THE PAST
AT SOUTHERN ACCENTS
ARCHITECTURAL ANTIQUES IN CULLMAN

Dr. Garlan Gudger, Sr., had a penchant for bringing home the treasures he found in old homes, churches, and businesses. In 1969, his collection outgrew his wife's tolerance level, so he opened a storefront in downtown Cullman. One storefront led to multiple storefronts, Gudger, Sr., convinced Gudger, Jr., to join the business, and Southern Accents Architectural Antiques is now one of the largest reclamation businesses in the South. If you are looking for the perfect touch for your new home or business, particularly an accent with a storied past, you are likely to find it here. The store contains a colossal selection of stained glass, doors, light fixtures, mantels, bathtubs, drawer pulls, knobs, sconces, chair legs, corbels, pipes from an old organ, and pretty much anything else that is of historical significance. The wood showroom at a different address has an abundance of reclaimed flooring, beams, and similar special finds.

Southern Accents is open Tuesday through Saturday and Monday by appointment.

308 2nd Ave. SE, Cullman, AL 35055, (877) 737-0554
sa1969.com

MAKE UP
A LUXURIOUS BED
WITH RED LAND COTTON PRODUCTS

Red Land Cotton has put Moulton, Alabama, on everyone's radar. The father-daughter duo of Mark Yeager and Anna Yeager Brakefield take the cotton they've been growing in Lawrence County for more than 30 years and turn it into exceptional bedding, bath towels, blankets, and bathrobes that can be shipped worldwide. Their new showroom and warehouse opened in February of 2021, so now it's possible to stop in and feel the difference for yourself that the red Alabama soil and using about a pound of cotton in every yard of fabric can make. You can see some of the cotton in the ground and the Yeager Gin just across the road. Mark and Anna feel that quality is assured as they "manage the process from the seed in the ground to the final stitch sewn." Some of the manufacturing takes place in South Carolina, Georgia, and Mississippi, but Red Land Cotton's 100% American-made products begin and end in Moulton. Look for the new showroom at the corner of Highway 157 and County Road 213.

1000 County Rd. 213, Moulton, AL 35650, (205) 235-9792
redlandcotton.com

MEET A POTTER
WHO IS A REAL MIRACLE IN VALLEY HEAD

At Miracle Pottery in Valley Head, Alabama, you will find pieces for sale that are intriguing, beautiful, and useful and meet the potter with a fascinating life story. Valinda Miracle is a descendent of the Cherokee tribe of Native Americans. She was a successful real estate agent before she suffered a serious head injury in an automobile accident. As part of her rehabilitation, she tried pottery and discovered a natural affinity for it, so she began to develop her skill. The results are wonderful works reflecting Valinda's spiritual beliefs. One of the most delicate is the Rebekah Pitcher based on verses from the Book of Genesis. Her kitchen items and dinnerware are completely food, oven, and microwave safe and come in an array of colors.

Valinda is a painter, the author of several books, and the owner of Treehouse Cottages that are available for rent on the same property as Miracle Pottery.

7871 AL Hwy. 117, Valley Head, AL 35989, (256) 635-6863
miraclepottery.com

SEEK OUT ANTIQUES, GIFTS, OR SPLURGES FOR YOURSELF OR A FRIEND
ON BANK STREET IN DECATUR

The Old State Bank Building dating from 1833 appears to hold court over all the happenings on Bank Street in Decatur. Storefronts and brick streets have endured for generations through times of waiting for riverboats to dock to streetcar days and beyond. The creak of weathered wood floors lends vintage vibes to the array of exceptional merchandise for sale on these three blocks.

Antiques take center stage with Bank Street Art & Antiques, 810 Antiques, and Tammy Eddy Antiques & Interiors, but you'll also find ladies' clothing at Threaded Boutique, custom framing at Behind the Glass, and fresh nutty goodness at Tennessee Valley Pecan Company. The Cupboard is one of North Alabama's only gourmet kitchen shops with the finest in gadgets and cookware.

Bank Street is a place offering quality goods in a time-honored setting and is a refreshing change of pace from big box stores.

Historic Bank St. NE, Decatur, AL 35601

SHOP FOR QUALITY FASHIONS
WITH THE DESIGNER ON-SITE AT BILLY REID IN FLORENCE

Billy Reid's first stores launched with his personal label were in Dallas and Houston, but his company headquarters is on North Court Street in Florence. His flagship store is on the ground level, and his design studio is upstairs. High-end fashions for men and women are displayed amidst antique chandeliers, mounted animal heads, well-worn but high-quality chairs and carpets, and other touches of elegance. Billy himself is often seen working inside the store.

Billy Reid was born in Amite, Louisiana, and spent time working in Texas, California, and New York, but he had the singular good fortune to marry a girl from Florence, Alabama, named Jeanne. The economic aftermath of 9-11 in New York forced him to head to Alabama, and Florence converted him and contributed to his success. He now has 15 stores and has expanded his line to include eyewear. Billy's designs are worn by A-list celebrities, and you could wear one, too.

114 N Court St., Florence, AL 35630, (256) 767-4692
billyreid.com

LOOK FOR TREASURES
WHERE GREAT-GRANDPARENTS SHOPPED
AT HARRISON BROTHERS HARDWARE

When you walk in the doors of Harrison Brothers Hardware in downtown Huntsville, you will step onto the same floors and view merchandise on the same shelves and walls that were in place when the doors first opened in 1897. The cash register that was added in 1907 will still be used to ring up your purchases. This is, in fact, the oldest continuously operating hardware store in Alabama. Harrison Brothers maintains the feel of a hardware store from days gone by. A selection of vintage toys like sock monkeys, marbles, and Raggedy Ann dolls are for sale, next to puzzles, foods, and products from local farms and artisans. Kitchen ware, such as baking pans and cast iron skillets, are offered near handmade soaps, candles, and coasters and relishes. You may be surprised to find prints and original artwork from local artists including Christian Wegman, Yuri Ozaki, and The Artlady, Sonya Clemons, along with jewelry, pottery, and books.

124 Southside Square, Huntsville, AL 35801, (256) 536-3631
harrisonbrothershardware.com

CHOOSE AUBURN OR ALABAMA ORNAMENTS
AT ORBIX HOT GLASS

Cal and Christy Breed have been impressing visitors with their fine glass art since 2002, headquartered in their shop at the edge of Little River Canyon Preserve near Fort Payne, Alabama. Their stunning centerpieces and jewel-toned glassware, vases, tumblers, and wall pieces are popular, but the collection of Auburn- and Alabama-themed ornaments never fail to attract the diehard faithful fans. Any self-respecting Tide or Tiger loyalist would be thrilled to have an ornament for their Christmas tree.

Orbix takes the month of August off for rest and repairs but during the remainder of the year, the gallery and hot shop are open Tuesday through Saturday. A regular class schedule is posted, so you can try your hand at this fascinating craft.

3869 County Rd. 275, Fort Payne, AL 35967, (256) 523-3188
orbixhotglass.com

TAKE PLENTY OF CASH AND SHOPPING BAGS
TO THE WORLD'S LONGEST YARD SALE

Imagine shopping your way through 6 states and 690 miles in only 3 days! That is exactly what happens the first weekend in August beginning at Noccalula Falls Park in Gadsden and ending in Addison, Michigan. Sales take place in front yards, pastures, side streets, empty lots, parks, and wherever you see 127 Yard Sale signs. That's because the route begins on Alabama Highway 127. There are no limits on what you might find, but most common items are antiques, collectibles, housewares, sporting goods, toys, tools, food, produce, musical instruments, furniture, jewelry, jams, jellies, and dishes. Many sellers will accept credit cards, but cash is best for bargaining.

Restrooms at major stops are either portable toilets or non-existent, so stop whenever you have the opportunity along the way. Most vendors open at 8:00 a.m. and don't close until dark. Treasures await!

127yardsale.com

TIP

The 90-foot-tall waterfall and the statue of the ill-fated Indian princess at Noccalula Falls Park are must-sees when you're in Gadsden. Trails, cabins, and a train ride add to the park's allure. 1500 Noccalula Rd., Gadsden, AL 35904, (256) 442-4960, noccalulafallspark.com

---

ANTICIPATE A SIGHTING
OF THE 1818 FARMS BLUE FLOWER TRUCK

During peak flower season, a distinctive, vintage blue truck makes the rounds in Huntsville, Athens, Madison, and Decatur bringing colorful blossoms grown on Mooresville's 1818 Farms to eager customers. Check the website to find the exact schedule and be aware that weather may change things a bit. Many of the 14,000+ blossoms are carefully preserved and used in arrangements available year-round, and if you sign up quickly enough, you can attend a Bloom Stroll & Bouquet Workshop where you will leave with a huge, fresh-picked bouquet that you have gathered yourself.

Natasha McCrary and her team have created a superior line of skin care products, dried flowers and herbs, coffee, candles, and more that can be ordered on Amazon or found at Southern Living retail stores or many other gift shops around the United States. Named for the year Mooresville was incorporated as a town, 1818 Farms is a picturesque, three-acre property on the northeast corner of the town. Demand for the products has almost eliminated scheduled tours of the property, but visitors are allowed to park outside the fence and peer over at the animals and colorful fields.

In 2019, Amazon named 1818 Farms as a Woman-Owned Small Business of the Year, so North Alabama is proud to claim it.

24889 Lauderdale St., Mooresville, AL 35649, (256) 489-0777
1818farms.com, facebook.com/1818Farms

STOP IN
FOR CREAM CHEESE
IN ELKMONT AT BELLE CHEVRE

The signs luring you off Interstate 65 in North Alabama are designed to create curiosity and stir hunger pangs. Belle Chevre cream cheeses made from goat milk are available in grocery stores, but it is so much better to visit the creamery for free tastings during midday hours Tuesdays through Saturdays. Fig and honey flavors have taken home numerous trophies, but other must-try flavors are garden veggie, roasted red pepper, coffee, cinnamon, and seasonal favorites such as pumpkin spice.

The creamery is housed in a former cotton warehouse beside the Richard Martin Rails to Trails tracks. Weekend tours, arranged by calling or making reservations online, include photo ops with resident goats, a film, a peek into the cheese-making kitchen, and a chance to taste the delicious products used in various ways. You're sure to leave with more than one. These tours are offered on Fridays and Saturdays at 10:00 and 1:00. While you're there, take a little time to stroll the adjacent trail along the railroad track and admire the 100-year-old warehouse that has anchored Elkmont for generations.

18849 Upper Fort Hampton Rd., Elkmont, AL 35620, (256) 732-4801
bellechevre.com

CELEBRATE OKTOBERFEST ALL YEAR
AT A TOUCH OF GERMAN IN CULLMAN

In 1873, the first German families arrived by train and made their new home where Cullman now stands. That German heritage is deeply woven into the personality of the town, many of its surnames, its historic district, its festivals, and traditions. A Touch of German was opened as a shop by Peggy Grobe in 1979 and is now owned by Judy Caples, whose mother is German and who was born in Germany herself. The walls and shelves are lined with Hummel figurines, German cookbooks, glassware, smokers, dolls, and, of course, cuckoo clocks. The shop even offers to repair cuckoo clocks.

Caples has added a wide selection of spices and teas from around the world and offers bread flown in directly from Germany every couple of weeks. It arrives partially baked and frozen, then you thaw it and finish baking it at home. I can personally attest to its deliciousness.

Oktoberfest is high season in Cullman, but Caples opens her shop several days a week throughout the year.

218 1st Ave. SE, Cullman, AL 35055, (256) 747-5737
facebook.com/A-Touch-of-German-Cullman-1979471902352809

ACTIVITIES
BY SEASON

SPRING

Look for Seasonal Delights at the Huntsville Botanical Garden, 79

Watch the Ever-Changing View While You Dine at 360 Grille in Florence, 32

Skip the Bugs and Sleeping Bags and Choose a Glamping Site Instead, 85

Learn the Impressive History of General Joseph Wheeler, 110

Take the Kids on a Scavenger Hunt, 86

Follow the Alabama Barn Quilt Trail, 74

SUMMER

Walk Down the Middle of the Streets on Friday Nights, 38

Order a Double Scoop of Orange Pineapple Ice Cream at Trowbridge's in Florence, 24

Join Thousands of Country Music Fans at Rock the South in Cullman, 41

Hang on Tight for a Thrilling Ride to the Mouth of a Cave, 48

Celebrate America's Independence at the Spirit of America Festival in Decatur, 63

Ride the Waves at the First Wave Pool in the United States, 93

Cheer the Trash Pandas at Toyota Field in Madison, 92

Remember a Brave Girl and Her Miracle-Working Teacher, 114

Take Plenty of Cash and Shopping Bags to the World's Longest Yard Sale, 136

Cool Off with an Upside-Down Banana Split at Kreme Delite in Athens, 18

Pick Ripe Fruits of the Seasons at North Alabama Orchards, 26

Anticipate a Sighting of the 1818 Farms Blue Flower Truck, 137

Listen to 10 Days of Music Honoring W. C. Handy, 54

• •

• •

FALL

Cross the Tracks and Celebrate Trains at Hartselle's Depot Days Festival, 36

Laugh, Cry, and Listen at the Athens Storytelling Festival, 50

Wear Your Toe-Tapping Shoes to the Tennessee Valley Old Time Fiddlers Convention, 62

Scare Up Departed Spirits on a Huntsville Ghost Walk, 64

Celebrate Oktoberfest All Year at A Touch of German in Cullman, 139

Pick Ripe Fruits of the Seasons at North Alabama Orchards, 26

Meet a Potter Who Is a Real Miracle in Valley Head, 131

WINTER

Catch Beads and Moon Pies at Carnegie Carnival in Decatur, 44

Observe Resident and Migrating Birds at Wheeler National Wildlife Refuge in Decatur, 82

Watch a Classic Film or Live Performance at the Historic Princess Theatre, 37

Spend 90 Minutes in Coolness and Wonder Below the Earth's Surface, 88

Explore Gadsden's Epicenter of Fine Arts and Creativity for All Ages, 101

Choose Auburn or Alabama Ornaments at Orbix Hot Glass, 135

Look for Seasonal Delights at the Huntsville Botanical Garden, 79

• •

SUGGESTED
ITINERARIES

FOR MUSEUM LOVERS

Acknowledge the Important Work of an Alabama Statesman at the Bankhead Home and Heritage Center in Jasper, 96

Catch the Passion for Huntsville History at the Huntsville Revisited Museum, 100

Gain Awed Respect for a Black Athlete Who Proved Hitler Wrong, 102

Grasp the Truth of the Scottsboro Boys' Ordeal, 106

Learn the Impressive History of General Joseph Wheeler, 110

Marvel at the Country's Best New Museum, 105

Sing Along with the Hits Playing Inside the Alabama Fan Club and Museum in Fort Payne, 118

Pay Tribute While Viewing the Symbols of Military Service and Sacrifice, 120

Discover Pope's Tavern Where Civil War Soldiers from Both Sides Were Hospitalized, 123

Take in the View at Burritt on the Mountain in Huntsville, 116

DATE NIGHT

Blend In with the Neighbors for a Meal at 1892 East Restaurant and Tavern, 6

Judge for Yourself How Chef Boyce Elevates Palates, 16

Hear Steamy Stories from the Past While Enjoying Stellar Dining at Simp McGhee's in Decatur, 33

Watch the Ever-Changing View While You Dine at 360 Grille in Florence, 32

Watch a Classic Film or Live Performance at the Historic Princess Theatre, 37

Enjoy Dinner and a Show at Von Braun Center's Latest Venues, 46

Relive the 1950s and 60s at a Drive-In Theater, 56

Rekindle (or Ignite) Romance at Gorham's Bluff in Pisgah, 113

Stimulate Your Senses at Tom Brown's Restaurant in Madison, 12

• •

FREE ENTERTAINMENT

CHEAP EATS

THE GREAT OUTDOORS

INDEX